The Essence of Death

EXIE SUSANNE SMITH

ISBN: 0692952403
ISBN-13: 9780692952405

Printed in the United States of America

DEDICATION

My Husband
With you all thing are possible, and because of you, I believe this. You keep me laughing, and help me stop my mind from thinking all the time. You are a truly wonderful man and life partner. I love you more each day. Thank you.

My Son
The one that never ceases to amaze. You are fun, funny and frankly, quite brilliant. You hug like no one ever has, or will. You bring joy. I love you to the moon and back. Thank you

My Father
You helped shaped me into the woman I am today.
You were my parent and became my wonderful friend.
I stood guard over you as you passed, as you stood guard over me as a child. I always felt safe. Your last earth-bound gift to me was allowing me to see your essence ascend home. I miss you everyday. I love you always. Thank you.

My Mother
You are the best cheerleader for whom a daughter could ever wish. You believe in me and my journey. That belief is the best gift you could have even given me. I love you. Thank you.

My Friends
You are my anchor. You push me to be more than I was yesterday. You make me laugh. I love you. Thank you.

My Readers & FollowersYou are the best. You allow me to follow my passion, to pursue my dreams. I do all of this for you. Thank you from my heart.

ACKNOWLEDGEMENTS

First Edition Edited by
Stephen Lloyd Smith

Second Edition Edited by
Cathy Plum

Cover Art
Brian Pilchowski
Edgemont Creative
www.edgemontcreative.com

Photographer
Jo Gifford
Firefly Photography
www.photofirefly.com

FOREWARD

After that first terrifying event, I started to journal. I never dreamt I would still be doing it 46 years later; the reality of this stopped me cold. Who does this? What has driven me to write? Was it my spirit guide with me, holding and directing my pen? I have heard, and felt in my gut, in this lifetime, the message that I am supposed to keep going … that this is all for a reason. It has led me to a place of happiness and contentment. I am blessed and thankful. This thankfulness covers a multitude of spirits, mainly my God. Simply stated, the Universe has conspired to bring me to this place.

This is the plan that was put into place long before I was born. I understand that I still have further to go, and much more to learn, before it is my time to rest. I am honored to have these abilities and to be able to help people until I take my last breath.

My goals, as I evolve and grow, steadfastly remain helping other people. Help them find their way, find answers within themselves, and to find peace and live the best life possible.

Thank you for joining me on these, the newest of adventures. I have unquestionably pushed the boundaries of my comfort zone, grown stronger, and witnessed otherworldly things. All this has changed the way I look at life, the living — the dead.

Come be a part of my adventures as we traverse the veil of vibrational energy in The Essence of Death.

CONTENT

Chapter 1

There's No Place Like Home

For me, home is where the heart is. It is the one place on earth where I am totally myself; safe, comfortable and able to recharge my energy. It is also a location with much spirit activity. I think there is no better place to start this new book than with tales of hauntings from home!

I am a lover of history. We learn from the past, so we should embrace it; that thought must be why I find the study of genealogy addicting. After much debate, I surrendered and joined a paid site to get information.

After several days of total submersion on the site, I noticed an energy spike in the house. The type of energy to which I am referring is spiritual energy. All sorts of shadow play were happening in my peripheral vision, it was as if spirit was pacing back-and-forth in my kitchen!

It never dawned on me that the spirits of my deceased ancestors would come to me simply by looking at our lineage. What I did not realize, at the time, was I must have been muttering their names as I read them. We must remember that what we put out into the Universe, is heard and acted upon.

These things are acted upon, and the resulting action may not involve only you. My husband had never seen or heard anything paranormal, and he was pleased with that fact; this was about to change.

It was a Saturday morning that consisted of a slow mellow start with coffee and no conversation. With coffee in hand, I settled on the couch to read a book. As I turned to my right to pick-up my book, I heard a noise. It sounded like a gasp or sharpe inhale of breath. Oddly, the sound came from the middle of the living room, midair. It was loud enough the our dog lifted her head in reaction in that direction. Just past the dog, my husband was standing in the kitchen. He looked up, "Excuse me, hon, what did you say?"

I turned to look at him, smiling, I said, "I didn't say anything. It seems, you have just heard your first spirit! What exactly did you hear?"

I heard you inhale, like you were going to say something, but didn't."

He was quiet for a very long time after that experience. I let him be, processing something like that is private. I was waiting to hear his thoughts on the event. It was only a sound—at least for him. For me, it was a brief flash of light, a shimmer of energy, then an inhaling of a breath in that exact spot. Spirits will find a way to communicate, often with less drama.

###

Christmas is one of my favorite days of the entire year, but this one is bitter sweet. It had been two years without my dad; it was his favorite holiday as well. It was Christmas Eve, I laid my head on my pillow and prayed to him, and anyone that would listen. "Please help make tomorrow special. Fill my heart with joy, like I used to feel on this day. Thank you."

When I awoke on Christmas morning, I rolled over in a groggy state, thinking I was hearing something. I laid there for a long time. I was hearing something—I was hearing sleigh bells. I slowly arose, and checked the window at the foot of the bed; it was closed. Listening, I tiptoed to the bedroom door, and out into the rest of the house. It was silent. Climbing back into bed, the sleigh bells continued to ring, apparently just for me.

I was full of joy; this was the best gift I could have received. I felt that this was my dad, and my spirit guide, conspiring to bring me such a joyous awakening.

This is recent and hard to talk about, but a beautiful example of spirit coming in to help, doing as we bid them to do. Our sweet dog, my daughter Lola, passed away. I had minimal warning that anything was wrong, but knew in my heart it was as planned. When it was certain that she was not going to live, I talked to my spirit guide, asking for support and guidance. Immediately I thought of my father, who passed several years ago. I asked him to please be the one to come down and carry our little girl home.

Within seconds, the energy in the house shifted, and I knew someone, in spirit form, was with us in the house—and I knew it was my dad. My son and sister-in-law rushed to be at the house with us. We were sitting in the living room holding Lola. I said a low thank you to my dad for coming so quickly. I considered this a private request between my father and me, for Lola. Knowing Lola missed him after his passing, she would be ecstatic to see him; that would be the only smile I could muster for several days.

The only proof I have that events did transpire this way for Lola, is in my mind's eye and heart. That's all I need. May God bless you both, I love you.

I sent two spirits packing today, the house is palpably calmer, less spirit pressing on us. The first was easy, he was ready to go home, so I helped him walk into the light. I had never done this—it was breathtakingly beautiful. The second spirit was not quite as easy; I had to banish him to the garage months ago. He was sealed in black plastic, with salt, and a Saint Michael medallion placed inside.

I could feel both spirits, all the time, around the house, but the latter was mostly in the back of the house. Even after I sealed him in the bad, he would get out and test the walls at the back of the house, trying to get back in. I would feel him first, then I would see him peeking at e. It was either from around a door or I would just see his head and shoulders through the wall. He thought he was stronger than me, simply because I went about banishing him, and not just throwing the framed picture I have of him in the garbage bin. People should never mistake nice for weak, it gets you in trouble every time. His attempts to get back into the house were growing tiresome. I learned that, even while in the front of the house, whenever I felt him enter in back, I could put my hand up and, with a pushing or punching motion, knock him back into the garage. I had finally learned how to seal the door—that kept him from coming back in.

My husband and I had planned, and set time aside weeks earlier, to clean the garage. The time arrived, and it happened to be the day after I had finally sealed my great uncle in there. I had items in the garage on which I desperately needed to make decisions, but I thought it best to delay. Sealing him in there had taken great time and energy. I knew my husband could come and go in there, without breaking the seal, but my doing so was a different story.

With no choice, the next morning I burst into the garage, ready to get my part done as quickly as possible. The spirit had other ideas; I was instantly dizzy from his energy. The most prevalent feeling I was picking up was anger. I had successfully sequestered him, and he was angry about it. I also felt confusion from him; he was wondering why I had locked him out of the house. I talked about this man, this spirit, in my last book. He was the great uncle I had never met. Before he passed away, he had gone insane from the effects of brain cancer. He did not go home, and instead he attached himself to a picture of him and his sister (my grandmother). There is no reasoning with him, he is quite insane, so I forcibly keep him out. I have tried to send him home many times, yet have failed every time. He does not want to go. I think he is afraid that God's opinion of him is bad. He changed religions, from Lutheran to Christian Science, and thinks God is mad at him for that. I have tried to explain to him that God does not work that way—well, at least not my God.

While I was sorting all of the stuff, I became lost in my own thoughts. It took me a moment to realize, but all the skin on my body was raised in goosebumps.

Standing up from the box I was going through, movement behind me caught my attention. Swinging back-and forth, in a wide arch, was a tennis ball on the bottom of a rope that I use to judge when backing in my car. The only way this could move is by force, by someone physically pushing it. For a spirit to make it swing on an arch this wide took a lot of energy. I stood and watched it in amazement, wondering if my great uncle had materialized behind me, as he manipulated the ball into action. As I processed the event, I noticed movement in an old mirror we had hung from a shelf, across the garage from where I was standing. Reflecting in the mirror was the fleeting image of my great uncle behind me. Turning around to face him, he rushed aggressively toward me. Just as he would have run through me, he disappeared.

Turning back around to see if he had, indeed, continued through me, I noticed the tennis ball, which should have stopped moving by now, was still swinging, just as wide as it was in the beginning. No way the tennis ball could have kept that inertia to create that high of an arc.

My conclusion of this event, was that the spirit reactivated the movement of the tennis ball after it rapidly went by me. He had not passed through me, as I would have felt his cold presence.

I stood watching the ball; it slowed, and stopped as it should have in the first place. I was also open, spiritually, to my surroundings; there would be no more surprises from my great uncle. Just as the ball came to a stop, I asked, "Will you come back and do that again? It was great, I enjoyed the activity!" Nothing more happened in the garage, however, I cannot say the same for in the house. My hunch was right. When I passed into the garage, I took down the block I had earlier put in place.

Still learning about the paranormal and the spiritual, I had believed what my great uncle said to me. He told me he would be good—and to please not send him away. I listened with my heart, not my gut. If I had listened to my gut, I would have known. He was only saying what I wanted to hear, this was not done.

Technology is a wonderful thing. Today I discovered I can get my new TV and computer to link up! My husband had been watching videos of car races and fishing, so why couldn't I find workout videos? It was frigid outside, so attending a workout class was not going to happen. I found several options for cardio dance, picked one and started to follow along.

Right in the middle of what I hoped would be a sixty minute session, I felt a spirit enter the house. As involved as I was with this video, the entrance and energy of this spirit was blatant and strong. I stopped my movements, which had me facing away from the TV. With a surge of energy and rapid movement, the spirit was right behind me. I made a motion, with my right hand behind me, signifying that I am closing the area behind me, while adding protection. Then, I told the spirit to get the hell out of my house and away from me and mine.

In a flash, I knew it was gone. Turning around to verify that fact, I saw a shadow of a tall, bulky man on the deck. He walked in front of the sun, so his shadow shown across the closed blinds on my living room windows. Quickly pushing up the shades on the window, there was no one around. He could not have got off my deck and out of sight that quickly. Also, as my husband pointed out, I would have heard him walking on the deck.

Such an odd, showy display of manliness from a dead stranger. I covered my house with protection and brought in guardian angels. It makes no sense, but then, what has in most of my life where the paranormal is concerned? I simply chalked it up to another weird moment in my life.

###

My mom called me on my cell phone, she sounded confused, which was disconcerting. She had something she needed to talk about—my concern did not lessen. What she relayed was the furthest thing from my mind. Different from any conversation I would have dreamt having with her.

She told me that last Saturday was the strangest day. I smiled, and thought you are not kidding. "I got out of bed late that morning and went to my bedroom door, but it wouldn't open. I pulled and pulled, it wouldn't budge. It did not seem stuck—it felt as if someone was holding the door shut by the knob from the hallway side—they were not going to let me open it. I gave up and came around through the door from the bathroom."

This was interesting, for several reasons, the first being the timing of the event. It was happening at the same time the spirit of my great uncle had disappeared from my garage. Second, every night I ask an angel to guard my mother's bedroom door to keep her safe. Had my great uncle appeared at her bedroom door, preventing her from exiting? Was she not allowed to come out into the hall because he was there, in a psychotic rage?

My mom continued with her story, "Later in the day, I went back upstairs to get dressed. I grabbed ahold of my bedroom doorknob, turned it, and walked right into the room. Just as I crossed the threshold, I realized the door wasn't stuck anymore."

I told her about my experiences in the garage, and my thoughts on the timing of her events. I confessed, too, about sending angels to her house every night to protect her; she was touched and thankful. After hearing all that I had to say, she came to the same conclusion I did: that my great uncle had shown up at her condo and the angel stopped him from entering her room, or stopped her from stepping out into his rage. We are not sure, but either way, she was saved from an event that might have severely frightened her.

My mother's odd morning did not end there. After she got dressed, when she went back downstairs, the phone rand as she entered the kitchen. "I looked down at the Caller ID and it showed my phone number, from here at the condo. My hand froze over the phone. I was honestly afraid to pick it up."

I asked, "Are you sure you were reading the correct number on the readout?"

Her startling reply, "The readout only has one number that shows up—the caller!"

"Did you answer it?"

"Yes, I wanted it to be your dad, I miss him so much; I wanted to hear his voice one more time. I didn't hear a voice, but the sounds coming from the phone were the oddest thing I have ever heard come through a phone. It was a hollow sound, an endless sound. Sadly, that was all, just noise, nothing else."

I was furious, but did not let my mom know how much. This had been the nasty work of my great uncle; how cruel this was. Shame on him for torturing a widow who misses her husband more than anything in the world. He is upset with me, and in his demented mind this might somehow force me to let him back in the house. That was laughable.

I heard nothing, nor did I pick up anything from my great uncle for almost a week. My mom said her electricity had been odd all week. I knew why, and that he was still there. I think he thought he would simply go back to the condo basement, where he had been for years. He did not remember his nephew (my dad) had passed away several months ago. Now his only blood family was me; I feel bloodline is important to him. Why? I have no idea. In my gut, I knew he would be showing up...back at the house any day now.

He refers to me as Susan. I have never gone by Susan and quite frankly never will. It is not me, but my aunt, his niece! It was such a moment of clarity for me, he thinks I am my aunt; he called her Susan when she was a child. He passed away when she was in her mid-20s, she had not seen him for years. My dad was about twenty the last time he saw his uncle alive.

I knew the moment he came back, I got so dizzy I almost fell over simply standing in the kitchen. Oh joy, was all I could think! I had worked on some ideas, a plan of attack; once he did show back up, I needed to help us both find peace. My goal was to try and get him back to some rational thinking, as much as possible anyway. The end goal in that was to send him home. He needed to know God did not hate him for changing religions. He also needed to know his family was not mad at him for not seeking medical help, which was against his newfound religion.

I started talking to him that day. I asked him if he missed his sister, niece and nephew, and parents. That got his attention. The battle of wills had begun, and would rage for weeks. My questions to him: "Why will you not even consider a conversation with your God? Better yet, how about a conversation with your sister? I know you two were very close, and I know, too, that she misses you." He told me he was angry and afraid—he was angry that God let him die, and so painfully. He thought his new religion would save him, heal him. He had fooled himself into this belief, he was angry at himself, and embarrassed. It frightened him when he found out he was sick, and what type of sickness it was. He had fought for his country and was now going to die for it. He had been mustard-gassed in the trenches in WWI. Many were affected in the years to come with sinus cancer that would spread, just as his had, which led to more anger.

My great uncle's slow death, and tremendous pain, drove him to madness. I cried from his imagery. This would have broken anyone. I was giving him the time he needed, bless his heart. I was feeling stuck in the middle, between a ghost and his God. I could only speculate how this had made him feel; the feeling of betrayal was huge. My goal remained steadfast: help him find peace so he could go home. If he went home, he would heal.

For several months, I talked to him—talked at hime really. I knew there were times he ignore me. I need to keep putting the message out there for him that he would be safe, that he was loved, that he would heal. It had now been six months. I felt it was finally time to try and get him to go into the light. Baby steps here, I mean what I say, people, baby steps are steps, too. I could feel his anger melting away after all this time. He was easier to talk to, I got a lot less static from his illness. The entire house was feeling more relaxed, instead of it feeling like it had just been hit by lightning. I still had him banished to the garage, I needed that for my and my family's energies. He would still slip into mental lapse, not communicate for days at a time. That was sad to see, and disheartening…I was becoming exhausted.

One night, I called upon God, Saint Michael, my grandma, and my father to come and collect him; to bring in the white light for him and gently lift him home, please. In my mind's eye, I could see a column of beautiful, warm, white light descend down into the garage. A hand reached out from an opening in the light—it was his sister, my beloved grandmother. He took her hand, and was just even with the sky, about to totally ascend, when he let go. She would not and could not force him to go. He was not ready, not convinced.

I knew he was back, and confused. He had slipped, yet again, into his oblivious mode. I was sad for him and disappointed for us both. He was so close to being where, I know in my heart, he should be. With his damaged mind, he did not see that.

Now, another year and a half later, he is still banished to the garage. He worms his way in about every six months through the walls, which I have to reseal. He can no longer can enter through the door that I sealed permanently! Things with him have settled. He knows if he gets out-of-hand again, I will have to send him away. I would hate to lose this photo of family; it is the only one I have of him at this age. Regardless, I will do what is necessary for my family's safety and health.

###

Exie Susanne Smith

Chapter 2

Lend a Helping Hand

My husband received a text from someone he fishes tournaments with: "Might need your wife's help, will let you know." He read that to me and sat back to digest. I chuckled at my husband, not the text. I took that seriously. I knew this was one of the last people he would have expected a note from requesting my assistance.

My husband is my biggest supporter, and I thank him for that. He surprised me one day with big letter decals down the side of his tournament style bass boat that says, "exieparanormal.com." He is proud of me, who I have become, and he believes in my abilities. I was shocked that one week after putting that on the side of his boat, he was contacted.

The next day my husband received another text from the same guy, "Need your wife's help. My daughter is seeing red eyes in her bedroom at night. What can we do? What is this?"

With concern and questions on his face, my husband looked at me. "Do you know what this is?"

"I have a good hunch, and it's nothing nice." It is not every day you hear that something is in someone's space, and it has red eyes. I suspected bad, but I did not want to make the jump to assuming evil. I assumed it was doing this to intimidate her, for effect, she is a 13 year-old after all.

This young woman and I had never met, however, I had heard wonderful things about her. She fishes with her dad, so my husband has met her on many occasions. He has always talked highly about how grown-up and level-headed she is. Plus she can really catch some fish!

Cutting-out the middle man, I had my husband ask for his daughter's number, so I could get her on the phone directly. I wanted to hear her voice, so I could gauge what I was dealing with, and how she was doing. As I tuned in, I could immediately feel and see, with my third eye, exactly what was going on. She had a spirit attached to her. I never saw this, but I knew to believe what I was seeing.

It was an old man latched onto her back, like she was wearing a backpack. His chin rested on her left shoulder, with his head pressed into her neck and ear. His arms encircled her, with his hands firmly grasping her breasts. Outraged and disgusted, I vowed to make this old man sorry he had ever touched her.

Suddenly a question came into my mind. "Have you been sick lately? Exhausted, having issues with your left ear and glands?"

She was shocked I had asked. "Yes, I have been sick for weeks. The medicine won't cure my ear infection. How did you know?"

I buffered the information, but told her what I was seeing attached to her. She seemed to take it in-stride, which pleased me. Working with someone not in hysterics is preferable. We set the day for us to meet at his house.

Having never dealt with a spirit attachment, and some-thing I suspected was evil, I sent out feelers to a couple mediums to see if one was available to cover my back on this. ...I also contacted a friend of mine, a demonologist, that lives in Traverse City, Michigan. She gave me some great advice about what to expect from an evil entity. She even suggested I watch a certain video that she had done on this very subject: spirit attachment and demons. I immediately pulled up the video; it was exactly what I needed, the down-and-dirty education on dealing with evil.

With the proper knowledge of what I was getting into, I almost canceled the other medium. I knew at this point I could take care of this on my own. Deciding not to do that, I started to gather the tools I thought I would need to cleanse her and the house. I had a huge bundle of sage for burning, oils to anoint, salt to lay and prayers to say as I used these tools. As I got ready to leave the house, I prayed for protection for all of us and our vehicles. Spirit can, and will, mess with your transportation in order to stop you from showing up. I called in God, my angels and Saint Michael to go into their house ahead of me and get things ready to cleanse. Using my abilities to check into their house, the demon knew we had talked. He also knew I was coming for him.

When I arrived, father and daughter were waiting for me outside on the front steps. The medium I contacted was going to be late. I knew the demon was watching me—and ready—the time was over for waiting. Collecting my items from the car, I joined them on the steps. I officially introduced myself and put out a hand to shake. I wanted to physically touch them while I simultaneously opened up. I needed to know what they were feeling, thinking, and if they were mentally healthy. They were both scared, confused, and had a healthy amount of skepticism.

I went into detail with them on what I thought was happening, and what I had planned on doing to rid the daughter, and the house, of this sick, old man. I used the word plan, letting them know that sometimes plans change as we peel back the layers of things. I took a minute to calm her father down, he was rightfully angered at this thing. I told him this thing wants your anger—it eats it for breakfast—so feel it and then get rid of it. We cannot go into the house until you are neutral on this. At this point, the father and daughter looked at each other. The father gave his daughter a quick nod, she turned to me and invited me in the house. Apparently, I passed muster! Now it was time to get to work.

Lighting the sage, I used it on her first, then the father. It did not get rid of the attachment, and I did not think it would. What it did was, loosen his grip some, and allow me to set my intentions of making him leave. He started to grumble in annoyance, I knew I was getting in. The sage, combined with the prayer I said over her, had him yelling obscenities at me and screaming in anger. I was hurting him, so I quickly set another intention; this one was so that he could not hurt her, or any of us, for that matter. He was furious with me and kept telling me so, in very descriptive language! With a bit more sage, and another prayer, there finally was a wedge driven between the two. We were so close to getting him loose, I hit him with a bolt of my own energy. He shot off oh her like he had been flung out of a moving car. He was weak, I set more intentions so he could not get another hold on her. Feeling confident that he was severely diminished, done-in, he knew that, too. He kept looking me in the eyes, calling me a bitch. I smiled at him, but did not reply. There was no point. I was thinking go ahead and use your energy, it will be over quicker that way.

He flew down the steps to the lower level, he was trapped. There was no hurry. I finished saging the upstairs, and somehow knew I would have to revisit the master bedroom. I was picking up something in there that I could not figure out.

Once I visited the lower level, it made sense. Before leaving the upstairs area we were working in, I had her father use the oils on the windows and doorways. I asked that he say some words to his higher power, then to dip his finger in the oil and apply it while making the sign of the cross in each place. He was happy to help. We saged our way to the lower level.

At that, point I salted the steps to keep him from getting back upstairs. Salt creates a great natural barrier against spirits, good or bad. It was a move to further trap him in a small area—which can get exciting. The young woman, whom I had stay near me, said, "I feel better; the house is feeling lighter. This is for real! Is he gone?"

Relieved she felt better, I looked at her and was honest, "He is off of you, yes. However, he is still in the house, and we are currently limiting his area. He is hiding from us, running for his survival. He will soon be gone, these were the first steps, just a bit more to do." What I found next would hamper our progress—but not destroy it.

"Let' finish this thing." As we descended the stairs to a full lower level, my chest got tight, it was hard to breath. He was starting to panic, and I was feeling it. That empowered me, I grew in conviction and confidence. My life was going to be forever-changed after this experience.

The young woman's room was down on this level.

Entering her room was like entering a cave, dark and cold. There was no natural light. I asked her, "Why is your window boarded-up?"

"It broke and my father hasn't gotten around to fixing it." That had to change, the dark loves the dark. This nasty spirit was flourishing in her room. I thought back to the text where her father said his daughter was seeing red eyes in the dark. Holy Mother of God, I would never have come back in this room at her age. She is brave and strong. The broken window is now on my mental list of things to talk to her father about.

Two steps into the room, I was immediately drawn to her closet. I asked, "Is this where you see the red eyes?" She shook her head yes. I could tell by the look on her face that she was shocked I knew that fact. Simple really, he left residual energy, a bunch in one spot; I knew that this was his spot. On the back-side of the closet was an opening in the drywall. Mentally, I questioned why it was there, assuming it was something else that just did not get finished. My abilities, once again, told me what I needed to know. I remembered seeing openings in other rooms of the house. This spirit used these openings as a tunnel system to travel all over the house and not be detected. He's a crafty bastard, I will give him that.

I saged her room; my chest was feeling a bit better. Next, we salted the opening in the closet, the window ledge, and the threshold into her room. Oil was applied simultaneously as a blessing was said. It was then I felt her room was safe. There were four other rooms in the basement—all were saged, salted and oiled. She asked if he was gone. I looked at her and said, "No, now he is hiding upstairs into your dad's room". He had used one of the holes in the wall to escape. I knew exactly where he was. Remember when I said I would have to go back to the master bedroom? Well, now I knew why.

Back upstairs, I went right into the master bedroom's ensuite bathroom. The shower stall had been saged, apparently not well enough. At the time, I had not noticed the opening in the linen closet drywall, consequently, that had not been saged. More sage, and this time salt into the opening in the drywall, plus we applied oil over the opening. As I saged, I could hear this evil spirit screaming at me: "You Bitch, I will get you." One last gut-wrenching scream and he was gone. I smiled and hugged my young client. She did not ask with words, her eyes did—I shook my head yes.

At that point, I noticed we had been joined by a woman. We were introduced to dad's girlfriend. I had to know, so I asked, "Did you get creeped-out, feel watched or not alone in this area of the bedroom?" I laughed because her face told me she was not happy with that question, a bit personal! "Sorry to ask, I know that is personal, but seriously, did you?"

Eyes wide with surprise, she said, "In fact, yes, I do and always thought it was just my being silly—my imagination getting carried away."

I pointed to the hinged part of the bathroom door, "That is where he used to hide and watch you. He was a creepy Peeping Tom, that is no longer. He is gone."

Just to be safe, I reapplied sage, salt, and oil to the master bedroom. It cannot hurt to layer-up, especially with this type of evil energy. Stepping into the living room, everything felt lighter and looked brighter; father and daughter mentioned it as well. I told her that now she has to let all of this go. Do not think about him; give him no attention or he will feel wanted and come right back as soon as he can. Let him go, it is over.

We started to gather all the items we brought with us, when we were asked if we could go right now to his ex-wife's apartment. It seemed she, too, was having some issues there. I had an idea of what he was talking about. He did not realize his daughter had already told me about some of it. Of course, yes. After getting into my car, I followed him several miles to the apartment.

As we parked our cars, I knew we had been sensed by whatever this thing was. In my mind's eye, I could see a little boy's bedroom, wherein a floating ghost was in the middle of the room, facing away. The minute my car's front tires touched the curb, the spirit spun around, now facing toward me, and looked right at me.

As we entered the basement apartment (I do not like basement dwellings), I saw a spirit walk through the kitchen, down the hall to its right, and directly into a bedroom I knew was the little boy's. It was done purposefully by the spirit, this was a show. It was saying to us, "I know who you are, why you are here, and I am not afraid of you." It should have been afraid, but I did not let-on with that fact. A dark spirit will use your ego against you. Be confident and strong, and leave the ego behind.

Introductions done, I asked to see the apartment. I wanted to see her little brother's bedroom, where I was told he talks to someone that comes into his room. Looking briefly into each room, I was staying closed to protect myself. I went back in the living room to let the mom know what I saw, and what had to be done. She gave us permission.

As I was saging the living room/dining room area, the daughter came to me to fill-me-in on the rest of what had happened here late yesterday afternoon. "My brother and I were here alone. I was in my bedroom next door. He was talking to something and I wanted him to stop, so I went in his room. He turned, looked at me with an angry face, I had never seen him make, and then yelled NO at me. His voice was not right, it was not his. I backed out of his room and as I did, I heard a really weird laugh."

By the shocked expression on her face, mom was hearing this

for the first time. She looked at me, "I also have an event that took place in my son's room." I was all ears. The more information you can have the better. She continued, "I got home from work, both the kids were in the living room. I put my grocery items down in the kitchen, and went down the hall toward my son's room. I was hearing voices, so I assumed he had left his TV on. Just past halfway to his room, I heard a voice say, "Come here." The voice was gruff sounding, then a crazy laugh. I immediately stopped, it scared the crap out of me. I kept going though, I knew I had to go in his room. I was so relieved that there was no one there. However it did feel like someone had been." After that, she gathered-up the kids and left the apartment.

I could sense that the mom had issues, I assumed drugs or alcohol, not sure to what degree—for my purposes, it does not matter. I know those things can cause you to hallucinate and create an opening for this type of activity. I also know that evil entities can bring you to those problem. What came first, the entity or the problem? With this new information, I proceeded with the saging. Either way, doing this was not going to hurt them, it would actually remove negative energies. Perhaps doing that alone would help them find some clarity.

Lighting the sage bundle, I headed straight back to the little boy's bedroom. As I entered his room the shadow, I saw enter his room earlier, rushed into his closet. The person with me said the back-wall of the closet appeared to have a portal in it. I was not convinced it had formed into one yet. I was not feeling it as one, and I would if it was open. I saged it, I would have done so anyway. You have to sage everything and everyplace, spirits and ghosts will hide anywhere they can to avoid the smoke of the sage. I also put intentions on the wall to make sure it stayed closed. As we filled the room with smoke, we cracked-open the window, allowing the smoke, and anything attached to it, a way to leave the room. We salted his windowsill and doorway threshold as we left the room. We saged the rest of the apartment, room by room, repeating the same process we used in the little boy's room.

When the process was down, I sat all of them down for a chat. I explained what was done, why it was done, and what we got rid of. I also told them that there might be some residual energy left from this thing for a few days. If they felt it any longer than that, they should contact me, and I would come back to do a second application. I also suggested that they not discuss this, especially in the apartment, and to let all thought of it go. The mom asked why. I explained to her, if you give it strength with your thoughts, it creates a doorway back in.

On my way home, it crossed my mind this situation, being what it was—evil, possibly demonic—I might be going back. Like everything else, time will tell. As I pulled in my driveway, I got a text on my phone. It read, "I am free!" I smiled, looked to heaven and said aloud, "Thank you. Please continue to keep this sweet, young woman free and all of them safe."

I have been taught that when you put a thought or wish out into the Universe, good or bad, it comes back to you. In this situation, I asked of my guide, "What was this thing that was coming after the little boy?" I read everything I could get my hands on, asked people in the field who have been out in the trenches, and no one had an answer for me. My problem was I assumed it was a certain type of entity, with a name like other entities'. I had logically, or I thought, concentrated my search that way.

Many months later, I sat down once again at the computer to try and figure out what this nasty entity was. Frustrated after about an hour, I looked up and said, "What do I call this damned thing?" Pushing everything aside, I went to make some lunch. While I ate, I pulled-up my DVR'd shows, and, as it happened, there was an episode of Travel Channel's Dead Files from the night before. I hit play. While the female medium was doing her part of the investigation, she talked about an entity in their location—this blew me away! She was describing, verbatim, the evil entity from the little boy's room in the apartment. It was, straight-up, a demon, no fancy name at all. When I was done laughing, I thanked the Universe for bringing me to my answer. The Universe is not always quick, but it is always listening.   ###

Blessings for a dwelling, that people are newly moving into, is something I enjoy doing. It is usually a happy, upbeat occasion with an excited family; however, that is not always the case!

A young woman I use to workout with reached-out to me in a text inquiring about house blessings. We had not seen each other for a while. She had left workout due to pregnancy. Her husband and I had met about a year before; they make a great couple. In the text, she told me they knew there was a spirit in their house, and everything was fine until they started to remodel. This is common. Some spirits do not like change, stirring-things-up in their space. Her words were, "The spirit has become obnoxious, and with our new baby, this activity has made us uncomfortable. We want it gone." I totally understand this; a baby changes everything in a household. She asked if a house blessing would do the trick. I replied, "It normally would, but in light of this new information, no, it will not. I am planning on a cleansing, with some extra protection thrown in for the baby's sake." That is why I would rather talk on the phone, I need to hear peoples' voices. She freaked out a bit at this information. I explained exactly what I planned on doing, with sage, blessings, salt, and oils. There was still a verbal shoe in the air, so to speak, on her behalf. I wanted to get into the house as soon as possible. Their situation was not going to get better on its own. Her hesitation was still there and then she said it, "Depending how much this costs, we might have to wait for the next paycheck." The shoe fell, it totally surprised me. I felt horrible that I had not made it clear, "This is done for free, always. If people want to charge you, walk away from them, they are not ethical." With that cleared-up, we set the date.

When she gave me directions to the house, I was surprised to realize she lived one street over from a friend's house that was in my first book. She is the dear one who passed from lung cancer. They had moved several years before, but still, what are the odds?

I arrived at the designated time, parked out front on the curb, and tuned into the house. I immediately picked up an older male spirit and, to my surprise, a second spirit, that of a male child. This was an unexpected detail; their energies had created the portal that I sensed in a basement wall. That was only a precursor to what I would find. You simply never know what else might pop up!

The vortex was feeding the energies of the older male; he liked how it made him feel. He was becoming cocky with power—the energy was like a drug to him. The homeowners, I was sure, were paying the price of his energy addiction; he was taking energy from them as well. Since they were already exhausted from having a new baby, work, and remodeling, they would have no idea that any energy left, was being usurped by this spirit. Still in my car, I closed the portal in the basement. I learned, about a year ago, that this is one of my abilities, it comes in handy. Closing the portal got the attention of the old male spirit. I was thankful his ego kept him from seeing that I had actually closed the portal. He thought I was weak, and he would simply create a new, stronger one.

I knocked on the door, and was met by the male home-owner, he looked exhausted. He let me in, and I was drawn to the kitchen where I put all my items down on the table. Off to my left were the basement stairs—that is where I really need to go—and as soon as possible. I like to start by chatting with the homeowner, getting their take on what is happening, seeing facial expressions and hearing their tone. Then, I explained what I would be doing and their parts in all of it.

The minute we were done covering everything, and he had no questions, I lit the sage bundle. It was at that time I realized I forgot to bring my large feather. Now what? I looked by the stove and asked if I could use one of the utensils. Feeling a bit silly, I grabbed the big pancake turner—I had work to do. Good thing there's no room for ego in all this!

I was off for the basement, burning sage, facing the pancake turner over the embers, with the homeowner in tow. Earlier, when I entered the kitchen, I saw the adult male spirit dart for the stairs, and could still fee him down there. The basement was exactly how I pictured it when I was in the car. I kept saging, high and low, all over the basement—making sure to get the wall where the portal had been. I told the homeowner that there was an adult male spirt hiding—he turned white. The situation changed quickly. "He just went up through the floor, he is no longer down here." Those words were just out of my mouth, when we heard running down the hallway upstairs. I was looking at the homeowner, he at the ceiling with his mouth gaping open. He whipped his head around to look at me, and said, "No shit!" I smiled, finished saging the basement, and we headed upstairs to finish this.

Back in the kitchen I said to him, "Both spirits are currently down the hall, one in each bedroom. The adult spirit is in your room, the one on the right, in your shower stall. The child spirit is in the baby's room, on the left, hiding in the closet."

He was blown away, "How do you know that? You are correct with which room is which, and that we have a shower stall, no tub." We looked at each other and simply started to laugh; that moment was a good tension reliever for him.

I saged the kitchen, then the den, adjacent that room, then down the hall. I went first to the master bedroom, directly into the bathroom. The trapped adult spirit was hit by the sage-smoke and was gone. Saging the rest of the bath- and bedroom, I crossed the hall into the baby's room.

As I saged my way into the room, I said a special prayer for this child spirit. I spoke softly, like a mom to her child, told him it was time to go home to his mother, and saged the closet. He had been on earth as a ghost for a long time. He had never gone home; a fact I did not realize until I got close to him. He went home with a happy little whoop sound. My eyes misted a bit with happy tears, he was no longer bound here. Clearing my throat, I told the homeowner both spirits are gone.

We finished saging in the office next door, and when the age put itself out, I knew we were done. I had the homeowner use the oil, with a peer and sign of his choice, over all the doorways and windows. I requested, too that he lay down salt all the way around the perimeter of the house to keep the adult spirit from re-entering. I could feel that the adult male spirit was already trying. He had died in a house close to theirs, and for some reason, chose to move in with them.

I was gathering my things to leave when the homeowner said, "I cannot believe how much brighter the house looks, it is crazy." It really did; it never ceases to amaze me. This is a clear indication if a job is done or not.

As I pulled away in my car, he was already laying the salt around the house—that spirit would not be getting back in.

###

I received a phone call from a good friend, fellow paranormal investigator, and spiritual medium, inquiring if I was available to lend a hand. A family with a newborn in southeastern Michigan requested help. My immediate answer was yes, even without checking the calendar. He went on to tell me that several family members had been scratched. Concerned that something might happen to the baby, they were finally driven to make a call for help.

My husband drove me down, he had business in the area, which worked perfectly. The apartments were a very old style, tiny, but clean, and seemed well maintained. I got out of the car and joined two others: the medium and the ghost investigator that set it all up. They explained to me they had been to this location a month earlier for the same issues. I did not let this sway my thinking in anyway, I cannot. You have to remain neutral until you are given a reason not to be.

We chatted outside the apartment by their cars, putting a plan together. The decision was, that first I needed to meet and get a feel for the client, whom they had already met. The second part of the plan was to deal with the entity, or entities, in the space. Gathering our tools, a prayer was said to protect us all. We headed for the apartment door.

An unexpectedly young woman answered the door, and invited us in. I immediately felt a rush of spirit come at us. The other medium and I looked at each other, simultaneously we gave a knowing-nod to one another. This was on! We stepped, literally a step, from the kitchen to the living room. There were two guys on one couch, two girls on another, and a baby on the floor with a tiny puppy playfully running everywhere! I was simply standing there shaking my head back-and-forth; this scene was utter chaos. My mind was reeling from what I was seeing and feeling. The spirit in here had a massive presence. The other medium was looking at me. He smiled and said, "I warned you!" I smiled back, shook my head again, we laughed.

The young woman that answered the door is the female that lives here, the mother of the baby and the puppy. The other people were her friends that come and spend days with her while her husband is working. She understandably does not like to be alone in the apartment.

I sensed, the minute she opened the door, that she had abilities. I also realized, in that instant, what was going on with her, she was open all the time (her crown and third eye)—an open invitation for everything and anything to come in. She had become a portal at this point. I also recognized she liked the attention it brought from family and friends. Her ego was creating a spiritual mess.

Looking at her crown, it was wide open, I shut it! She flinched with shock at the sensation, but opened it right back up with a satisfied smile. She did not realize what I had done, so I closed it again. Same reaction, with the same result. Honestly, I was not sure what to expect. Everyone followed her a few steps into the bedroom. Wham! My knees buckled. Dizziness swamped me, I had stepped into the middle of a vortex!

This tine bedroom had two portals, one in each corner of the room, opposing each other. In the center of the room was a tornado of energy, a fully formed, strong vortex. We stepped back out of the room to catch our breath. That is when I realized there was also a portal in the conjoining living room and kitchen wall. I made the assumption that the portal went all the way through to the kitchen. Stepping around the corner, I verified that it did. This tiny place was alive with spirit activity, more than this young woman ever imagined was possible.

I stepped back, into the living room, next to the other medium, facing the young mother. It was time for a so-called "come to Jesus talk." I began by telling her who I was, then into the history of Mediums, and her responsibilities as a part of a community. What you do represents us all, so be wise with your abilities.

She was speechless, and I wished she had stayed that way. I was just getting warmed-up, when she rudely cut me off and was flippant to me. She started telling me, "I'm not hurting anyone and these are my abilities to do with as I please."

I let her run on for a few moments, then I looked her dead in the eyes, raised my hand over her head, with a snap of my fingers shut her crown—none too gently. Her eyes were huge as she looked back at me. "Oh," came out of her mouth just before it audibly snapped shut.

I smiled at her and continued what I had been saying. "That is how your crown feels closed. If you keep it open all the time, you become exhausted, and call-in all manner of ghosts and spirits. They can be good or bad, in your case, bad. Get to know how it feels closed."

With his beautiful feather, the other medium artfully started moving the sage into every possible nook-and-cranny in the room. The sick feeling was losing some of its hold, a good indication that the sage was doing its job. The closet in this room is where this nasty spirit liked to hide out. He had traveled here using the attic to get into other apartments.

He said it a total of three times to me. At this point, I turned to the other medium, who was grinning at me; he had heard it, too.

I said, "I guess this thing isn't a fan of my work!" We laughed and kept on saging and praying. As we continued saging, the nasty spirit continued to berate me. Not sure why he thought I cared.

The room grew quieter still, the dizziness was now gone. We moved into the bathroom to do the same process, but we added salt so we could seal off the areas. You do not want a spirit to move back into a room you have already cleansed. Following the sage with salt, we finished the bathroom and the attached closet, where the HVAC system was located. It hit me like ton of bricks. I said aloud, "Oh my God! This thing is using the ductwork to move around the apartment!" I salted the vents and even threw salt into the ducts themselves—he was not using them anymore.

With these two rooms cleaned and sealed, we moved to the kitchen. As I stepped from the bedroom, I put salt down on the threshold. This thing was now totally cut off from those rooms. Turning from the doorway, we heard (telepathically) shit, shit, shit. The other medium and I laughed. He said to me, "You make him mad."

I replied, "Its a skill!" We were shutting-down this thing's world—and he knew it. He knew he was no match for us, and the goodness we were bringing to this place. Since I was right there, I closed the portal in the living room, then salted the area. We stepped into the kitchen, more sage and salt. I also closed the other half of the portal wall in the kitchen.

We did a final prayer for the location and the inhabitants of the apartment. Finally stopping to really take a look around the tiny apartment, there was so much sage-smoke, it looked a hazy morning over a major city. You had to bend forward to see under the layer of smoke!

I told the other medium I was going out to lay salt down around the perimeter of their apartment. It was the final touch of our process, another later of protection from spirit. Stepping back into the apartment, I knew the spirit was gone. I also knew he had simply moved next door to that apartment. I asked who lived there; it was a very sweet older woman that the young mother was concerned with. The other medium and I turned our minds to that apartment, and drove him out of there, with the stipulation he never return. He was very weak at this point, easy to manipulate. Also I got the feeling the neighbor had nothing to offer him, he would not have stayed long.

He was out of the apartment, blocked from ever returning. That was great, but we still had the issue of the young mother flaunting her abilities. I had decided that some tough love was needed to reinforce how vital it was for her to learn control. In the forty-five minutes it had taken us to cleanse this tiny place, I had closed her crown three times. Each time she gave me a sheepish look—my returning look was anything but sheepish.

The other medium and I had worked very hard getting the home back into their control. In this process, I had been told this was their second time here, not cool. I walked over to where the young mother was standing, "We have worked very hard to rid your home of a demon you invited in." She started to argue with me. I put my hand up and kept talking. "No, you have by choice stayed open, you brought him in. You were very lucky this situation did not get to a tragic point." Her eyes were huge. "I think its goal was to do harm to one of you, most likely starting by killing the puppy. It would then destroy your marriage, eating up your anger, growing stronger, making it into energy. With the two of you no longer strong and united, it would have been easy then to kill you off one-by-one."

She immediately apologized for playing a game with her abilities just to get attention. She hated being alone all day while her husband was at work. We hugged, I blessed her, her family, and the home on the way out the door.

UPDATE: The people that contacted me to come assist sent me a portion of the note the young mother sent to them. "It has been four months since you all were here, things are great. Thank you. I am getting more in tun with my abilities and my surrounding. That has kept things calm and settled. I am thankful, too, because now I understand what had been happening to me, and around me, my entire life. I now know why I know things I shouldn't. I am practicing how to turn these abilities on and off."

It is not often that you get a note, or any sort of follow-up. I am glad she took the time to let us know how things were going. I am proud of her.

###

Renting a house on vacation is relatively new to us. Since we rent for one month at a time, it is far less expensive than a hotel, and gives us much-desired space. We go to Clearwater Beach, Florida—this is the second year, same house. Last year I picked up on three spirits in the house. The first was a gentleman, whom I believe was the first owner, possibly the second. He looked like Fred Astaire, the famous dancer and actor. I only saw him once but felt him around several times.He loved that house and the location. The second spirit I saw was a woman; she was tough looking and tied to the third spirit, whom I'd felt, but had not seen. She struck me as a type of woman that liked bad boys, she dressed like a gun moll of the 1920s and 30s. The third spirit, male, showed up a bit later the same day. He was dressed as a typical gangster of the same era as his moll. I found it interesting that her message was he is mine, but his message was well hello, doll!

I could feel the previous renter, whom had left just that morning. I knew that energy would dissipate in a day or so, which it did. The other three energies did not. In fact the male ganger's spirit energy stayed very strong. That evening as we lay in bed, my husband and our dog, Lola, were sound asleep, I knew we were being watched from the hallway just outside the door. It was the gangster, simply standing there watching us lie in bed—it was creepy. I asked my spirit guide, in a whispered voice, to come protect us while we slept and keep this energy out of our room. That was good but not good enough. I got out of bed and closed the bedroom door.

The next morning upon waking, I looked right at the door, it was open. Then, I relaxed, realizing my husband and the dog were already up! I laid my head back down and thanked my spirit guide for protecting us all night. Having felt safe and unbothered, I had slept like a log.

I got up and headed for the coffee pot. Greeting my husband, who was watching morning TV in the living room, as I passed by on my way to the kitchen. Coming back, I sat on the couch with him and asked how he had slept? "Great, and all night; I never sleep all the way through the night."

Strange,I thought, either he or the dog has a duty call. "I worried a bit, having closed the door in the night, you might not realize it and walk into it."

He turned and looked at me, "Are you sure you didn't dream you closed it?"

"What? No, I closed it. You two were snoring away."

"Hon, the bedroom door was wide open when I got up this morning!" My entire body flushed with goosebumps. So much for thinking we had been unbothered.

As I moved through my morning around the house, I knew I had to try to figure this out. Sitting down in the living room, I closed my eyes and slowed my mind, trying to tune in to the house and its inhabitants. Right away I picked up a male energy. He is nosy, inquisitive, loves this house, lived in it many years ago. He loved the area, had money, and was an easy-going guy. Opening my eyes, the Fred Astaire look-alike spirit was standing on the other side of the room, smiling at me. He wanted me to know him, that he had been here, and he means no harm. As we stared at each other, he looked to my right into the hallway. He looked back at me, gave me a sweet grin and a wink of an eye, and he was gone.

I was feeling and energy off to my right, another male. I got up from the couch, walked to my right, now facing the hallway. I focused my mind on that spot. Feeling energy form into a mass, I opened my eyes—there he was, my Peeping Tom spirit. Age wise, he looked to be in his forties, dressed in a dark suit with white pinstripes and wide lapels, cuffed slacks, and a hat cocked down in the front over one eye. I was looking at a quintessential gangster, so cool! He gave off a creepy vibe—a male chauvinist vibe—women were for cooking, cleaning and sex sort of vibe. I was not about to allow him in my space, certainly not anywhere near me while I was defenselessly sleeping. I told him that we now had rules for this house. He was dead, I am the living, and that gives me all the cards for rule-making.

He gave me a smug look, like we'll see about that, and he was gone. I immediately pulled-in my spirit guide for a discussion. I brought-up needing protection from him—at night. I needed her and other angels to surround us in our bed, to help bring a sense of peace, and help keep the bedroom door closed while we sleep. I chuckled at this, shaking my head, thinking we shall see indeed!

That night everything was fine, I felt watched, but safe and most important, the bedroom door stayed closed. In the morning (honestly most of the day) I had a persistent feeling that there was more to this house, spirit-wise, than I was currently picking up. Stepping from the house into the attached garage laundry room, it felt crowded; it was odd, and felt as if several people had just left this area. I quickly glanced around the entire area to see if there was truly someone in there. I noticed, which I had not before, that the HVAC system for the house was built over the living room. The garage and attic of the house were all open, something we do not do in the northern part of the United States. It struck me that this was where the spirits stayed most of the time; I could feel three of them presently in that space.

Bringing myself out of my own thoughts, I put the dirt towels in the washer and went back in the house. It was almost lunch time. My husband had gone to the beach to fish, so Lola, my god, and I were on our own. I rattled a dish and the ever hopeful Lola came running to the kitchen doorway. Putting a few things on a plate, I was moving around the kitchen talking to her. It was weird, while I was talking to her, she turned her head and glanced over her shoulder into the dining room. I followed her gaze and we both saw the male spirit in the black pinstriped suit materialize. He was about a foot behind her. He looked a her, then at me. He then walked through the dining room table and the closed French doors of the sunroom. He did a half-glance over his shoulder, to see if we were watching, then disappeared. Without missing a beat, Lola turned her gaze back to me—Mom, let's eat!

Days have now passed, the spirits were behaving, keeping to themselves, which was great. I had planned on booking phone readings while here, but wondered if this would stir them back up?

I posted on social media that I was scheduling phone readings only. I thought if no one contacted me, then I was worrying for nothing. Checking my social media page later that day, I had six people that wanted a reading! Looks like I was going to see what the spirits thought about having a medium in the house.

The day arrived for the first of the scheduled readings—I was a bit nervous. My spirit guide came in, reassuring me that everything would be fine, as it should be; the support of that comment was all I needed. I am where I'm supposed to be, all is well.

The first reading was thirty-five minutes of pure love and fun. This woman's spirit family was a blast and very excited to be getting their messages delivered. She heard from everyone she hoped to. That is not always the case unfortunately. My hope was that all the subsequent readings were this wonderful.

The spirits were fine with me reading in the house (daytime was never a problem) it was nighttime that brought out the

Peeping Tom. He was a work in progress for me. I would not have him watch me sleep.

Another reading the next day, this one taught lessons, to both the client and medium. I had a sport come through with a message that the client said no way it fit the person. I had been hesitant to say what it was, and questioned myself for doing so. The rest of the reading went great, she was very happy, and that's all that matters.

The next day I got a message from her, "What you said about my family member, what I said didn't fit—well, I called my parents, and they told me it fit perfectly! I guess I don't know everything about my family, past or present." I thanked her for letting me know, and that it was kind of her.

I needed to look at myself. I had not believed in the message I had received. The self-doubt must stop. I will give the messages I am shown, with all the details that go with it. Just because it's nothing to me, does not mean it is meaningless to them. No matter how small, or odd, I have to tell them.

Days later, another reading, and another person that had no idea about something one of her family spirits was talking about. The spirit showed me a picture, well, a photo with a white frame around it. It was like pictures from the 1960s and 1970s, with a white scalloped edge. I now know that when spirits show me this image, the client has a picture of what we are talking about, be that a person or a place. Often the client will argue with me. I smile, because I believe what spirit is showing me. Often times, at a later date, I will get a message about a reading: "I found the picture!" or "my parents knew exactly what you were talking about and pulled out a picture I had never seen before!" They learn something good, and sometimes not so good, about family history.

I am being shown things in order to deliver that message or impress upon this person; spirits always have a reason for doing so. That is not for me to judge or interfere with, just deliver and move on.

That night as I laid in bed reading, I got the sudden feeling there was someone standing in the doorway to the room. My husband and our dog were sold asleep next to me. The book was up in front of my face, blocking my view—I was hesitant to lower the book! Slowly I lowered it to my chest, I could see a hat, then a face, etc. There was a male spirit standing there, staring at me. It was the same man in the black pinstriped suit. I could see through him—it was a bit of a relief that he was not alive. He continued to simply stand and stare at me, so I used that time and studied him right back. His appearance still blew me away. He was straight out of the gangster-era. He wore a hat, white shirt, black tie, and he oozed confidence. Being well groomed was important to him, his ego.

As he stood there, both of us still staring at each other, my chest started to get tight. I knew, then, that he had died of a heart attack, in this room. It made more sense to me why he stood guard on this location. It could also be that he still sees his era and we are intruding on what he thinks is his space.

I watched as he faded away, any sense that he was there was gone. He was on display a long time, he had to have exhausted himself. Reaching over I turned out the light, leaving the door open. I figured he would be too low on energy to bother us much tonight. I was not going to find sleep for a while anyway.

I told my husband, over breakfast, about the gangster spirit-visit last night. He just shook his head at me, "I love you."

After that visit, he never appeared to me again. I could feel him though. I did continue to keep the bedroom door shut tight. When we simply pushed it closed, and happened to wake in the night, the door was open. If it wasn't opened all the way, then it was just enough to see into the room. You could see his outline in the dark, just outside the door, simply standing there, not cool!

It will be interesting to see what happens with spirit in the coming year at the rental house.

Honestly, they need to be sent home, but I am not sure it happened—maybe I am the one to do it—I will ask them when we return next year.

###

Exie Susanne Smith

Chapter 3

Tables are Turned

My life has been one long ghost and spirit investigation. It has been a continuous series of events on a daily basis. These events are not limited to my home. They appear to me in other peoples' homes, in other states and even in other countries.

Their appearances are something I count on happening, and because of that fact I have been forced to grow my abilities. I can now sense them before they officially appear.

I have taught myself several ways to protect my home and me and my family. I can now, also, stop spirit from rudely dropping in, where ever I am.

I would never have dreamt there would be a day that I would be turning the tables on spirit, and appear without warning on them! Taking ownership of our lives is a must—for all of us; for me, it was a matter of survival. Especially when you have abilities and powers that you have yet to realized.

###

Laughingly I wanted to call this chapter, A Hunting We Will Go! These are the sorts of adventures at a strange new location, that I thought I would never be a part of. I watched an investigation team on a ghost hunting show on TV, they talked about not investigating alone. And, that it could be dangerous. Mostly, their point was someone could get hurt, and not be able to get out of where they were. That fact alone (forever, I assumed) put an end to my dreams of paranormal investigating.

I published my first book and booked myself a couple of author events. One morning, browsing the computer on social media, I came across an event called a ParaCon. I had no idea wha the health's could be, but was immediately intrigued. I found, on their event page, that for a fee you could be a vendor at their event. I signed-up and mailed-off my money. I showed-up in Sault Ste. Marie, Michigan with my husband, a few table decorations, and first my book. Over that one weekend, my life was forever changed!

There I sat, with my one book at a six-foot table, shy, blown-away by television and movie celebrities, and praying I would sell some books! I was meeting people from all over the country —the world, really. I talked with people that were part of a Paranormal Investigation Team. I learned that these teams go into homes and assist families that need help with the paranormal. Helping people is my path—this would be a way I could change lives, possibly save lives. My mind reeled for months after this, the possibilities were endless… I needed to be a part of a team.

Helping families in their homes happened quickly after the convention. I got a call from someone who had purchased my book; they needed help with a pesky spirit. These events, I did do alone, but the families were home, so technically not alone. My only tools were my budding abilities. Things went fine, I did not create more problems than they already had, luckily. I have witnessed this from others and vowed to get the education I needed to be better for clients. I have been fortunate to have been friended by many in the field. There are two people, in particular, who have given me great direction in this area; I cannot thank Brian and Marilyn enough for taking the time to do just that.

The tables have completely turned, I now go, confidently, in search of the dead.

Conventions and parafests have become a staple in my life. Excitedly, in 2016, I was going back for a third time to the Old Mill Parfest—a fabulously historic and haunted building. The preceding years, I had a vendor table only. This year I was vending, and had been invited to be a speaker. A proud time for me, I had proven where hard work can bring you.

The Old Mill sits on a river, the water runs quickly as it heads to a set of falls just past. This makes the building in itself, for me anyway, feel charged with energy. Now add in the other vendors, who many have psychic/medium abilities, and then add in the excited mass of people that attend. The energy is off-the-charts! As always, because of this, I keep myself heavily protected and covered there. If I don't, I am exhausted much too early in the day. Happily, the adrenaline of seeing everyone keeps me charged for ninety percent of the day, it's great!

New this year, I was invited to participate in the investigation at the end of the event. I had never investigated the mill. I had only heard the amazing experience of others. I packed up my table items, having excitedly waited all day, the greeting, selling, speaking and counseling were over. I helped gather the ticket holders, it was time for the investigation.

All participants gathered in the main hall, speakers were assigned locations that we would stay in for the entire time. Above the noise, they announced where the speakers were to be located: "Exie you are in the basement!" The shocked rumble of response from the ticket holders in the room was great, I laughed. We, the speakers, went to our locations as they divided the ticket holders into groups. The groups would come for a set amount of time to each location, investigate, and then switch out for the next group.

My assignment in the basement was with another speaker. He

asked, "Have you investigated here before?"

I looked at him, "No, never. I have heard plenty of scary stories from people. I'm not worried about it, I have been in haunted locations my whole life." He smiled at me, then we descended the stairs into darkness.

The basement is reportedly overrun with ghosts. I was excited to see if this was true. Some of the basement spirit activity I had heard about included people being touched, a spirit that likes to get right in the face of women, shadow people peeking around corners, and extreme cold spots. I had not been on an investigation for a few weeks, so I was ready to get things rolling.

We heard our first group noisily clamoring down the stairs. I could feel their nerves from fifty feet away. We waited for them to settle a bit, then had them get into a circle in the main room at the bottom of the stairs. I had been talking to my basement partner, when I looked around at the circle of wonderful people, they were all staring at me! A smile came over my face —this could only be one thing. I told them, "Not to worry, I've got this. The basement does not scare me. In my lifetime, I have seen so much." The gasp of breath emitted by one woman was a surprise. I was touched by her concern.

Not wanting to waste more of their investigation time, we explained how it was going to work, and what we expected. In a public investigation, you get all levels—from never having investigated, to the well-seasoned. It is good to even the playing field as best as you can. My goal was for as many people as possible to have a paranormal experience.

In the circle, my partner started with a question posed toward the dead, and the night officially started. I had my personal recorder running and, as always, I used myself as my main tool for investigation. There was plenty of investigation equipment being used. If beeps and flashing lights were what they wanted, that's exactly what they were about to get! As I felt spirit milling-about in the area, I would let the group know. It is fantastic when I let them know we have just been joined by a spirit, and then their equipment goes off—we all have fun then!

We next moved to an adjoining room, maybe twelve feet away. This room had a totally different feel; it was damp, full of cobwebs, and pitch black. You honestly could not see your hand in front of your face. This area was also loaded with spirit. Some ghosts had been hiding from us in there, while we were in the other room, but others were excited to see us, and joined in.

Tuning in to more spirits, I wanted to get an idea of the number of them and what they were about. I needed to keep the guests safe. I picked up on several male adults, two children —one male and one female. The adult male spirits were peeking at us from a room on my left, that went under the stairs, and a side-room off to the right. We placed an EMF detector in the doorway on the left, it lit up and stayed that way. The two kids were great; they would run through the room to make equipment light up and make noise. They were kids being kids, even after death. Weirdly, my heart was glad to know.

The nervous conversation between a couple of people was starting to get to me. It made me lose concentration, and touch with spirit. Glancing around, the spirits had all gone. I knew the kids were now upstairs (we bored them). I was bummed, but understood. I told my partner, "Well, the spirits are leaving and hiding, these people need to give them their attention." He laughed.

Half the group still had a death grip on each other, they needed to relax and stop talking. I had an idea, a diversion, to get them into it so they could have fun. I put several pieces of equipment on the floor, in the center of the room, and asked spirit to come in. I then told the group to ask questions: Who are you? Why do you stay? The group started relaxing and getting into questions. It was then spirits timidly started peeking at us from the other room. I could feel a male spirit approaching the REM Pod that I had placed (apparently a bit too close) next to a scared couple of women. Chuckling to myself, the woman next to me said, "What are you seeing? What's so funny?"

I did not get a chance to answer before the REM Pod made its horrid noise and one of the women screamed. All the spirits bolted from the area and hid again. After the nervous laughter settled down, the suggestion of what not to do was covered again!

It took another ten minutes of questions, directed toward the spirits, before they came back. I had to give them credit for coming back in, not sure I would have. I thought this time around, it might be good to give the group a bit of a warning that spirit had decided to grace us with a visit. Spirits hovered near doors and side-walls, and they did come closer. We asked more questions, with hopes that someone in the group with a recorder would catch an EVP. Everyone had settled down, they were using their equipment, snapping pictures, asking questions, and having a fun time. It was exciting to see them turn this into a great experience after such a rough start.

We moved the group into a third room—the final room—because their time was about up. I felt the spirit of the two kids come back into the basement, and I let the group know they were back. Just after I spoke, my basement partner asked, "Exie, you feeling all right?" He was using an infrared camera, and evidently had it pointed toward me.

"Yes, I'm fine. Are you seeing the cold spot that I am feeling moving behind me?"

"I am, it creeped down the wall and is currently…"

I interrupted him, "Climbing up the back of my legs, as we speak?"

He laughed, "It is, and you are so stinking calm!"

Deep in concentration, I had not realized most of the group had moved over to his screen, and were watching what I was feeling. They were shocked that I could just stand there. I knew it was not going to hurt me, not sure how, I just did. The cold feeling moved just below my butt, then reversed direction, headed back down my legs and then disappeared. We thought it might follow the same path—going back across the floor and up the wall—but it didn't. I said, "Well that is interesting. It did not go back the way it came?" No one answered. Not a problem, I had not really directed it toward anyone, maybe no one had an answer.

A few minutes later there was a cold gust of wind that came between myself and the woman standing next to me. It was a male spirit; he appeared right in front me and zoomed intentionally in my face—stopping only inches from my nose! He was trying to scare me, I'm sure, but it only annoyed me. I imagine he was disappointed! I found out later that night that this is one of the claims happening to women in the basement. I don't even like the living to be that close—let alone the dead —in a pitch dark room.

Off to my left and up a bit, was a doorway into another room. Looking into that room was like looking into black ink —nothing in the room was distinguishable. I knew a spirit was there, just inside the door jamb, I could sense him—and others.

I directed the group's attention that way, and they started to ask questions directly to that spirit. I was not sure he wanted to be seen, until he did the coolest thing. In the bottom half of the door, a leg was lifted up and out, like a Rockette dancer. The group quietly went nuts, it was so cool. I was chuckling, thinking who knew we had a dancer in the bunch? A voice came out of the dark from someone in the group, "Did I just see a leg?"

The group, in reply, "YUP!"

Then there was an arm stuck out, just the arm. Then a head appeared, just the head, no shoulders. I did not say then, but I thought that it was odd to see just the head. I did not need this group getting scared again.

Turning my head, I asked the woman next to me, "Are you cold?"

With a chatter in her voice she said, "I'm freezing, but only my legs."

From out of the dark, my basement partner piped-up: "That cold spot is back, but it's on the woman next to you."

The confirmation was fantastic. I loved that she did not panic; she stood there and let it happen. Once again, it went back down her legs and disappeared.

Group after group, four in total, came and went from the basement. Activity was high and, thankfully, stayed high all night. I found it interesting that the two little kids' spirits left the basement during the first group and did not return.

After the event, I found out that the kids followed, and stayed and played games with, the first group we had the rest of the night. That was quite a night, the Old Mill did not disappoint. The sprits were excited for the company! They were nosy and kind to all their guests. Thank you to all, the entire event was fabulous.

Conventions for the paranormal are one of the most fascinating things I have ever been involved with in my life. They draw a vast array of people from all walks of life and economic levels, which fades away the minute they come through the doors.

These events are some of the happiest hours I've spent. It is a time when I can talk about all of my favorite weird topics in this world, and beyond, with everyone in the room. This is not something I can do in everyday life. It is not like I care if people think I am crazy, it's just that they simply do not understand what I am talking about.

This particular event, held in mid-Michigan, is at an old building that has two spirits. These two spirits are complete opposites: good and evil, helpful and hurtful. The first time I was at this location, I was so dizzy I was not sure if I was going to be able to stay. There was a pull in the room that I had yet to understand. After a few minutes, the good spirit made an appearance. He came down the side steps of the stage, stopped at the bottom, looked around and went back up. Across the room there was a ramp that led to the restrooms and backstage. This area had a totally different feel—not a good one; it was creepy, heavy, and you knew you were being watched and judged. I knew I needed to stay away from there. I would figure out the restroom situation when needed!

Associated with this event, is a dinner and ghost investigation afterword at a haunted bar/restaurant. The upper floor of the place, at one point in its history, was a brothel. Not surprising, in the rooms upstairs are female ghosts, and also several male ghosts. The first one I encountered was such a worrywart! He did not like us up there, it made him nervous. He kept questioning, "What are you doing up here? You are not supposed to be up here." The second male spirit was a very bad man, evil feeling. He had done bad things to the women who were employed there. I first picked up on one child, then a second in the hallway area upstairs. The evil male spirit had hurt them as well. The child spirits were frightened by him.

The busyness of some, mixed with the craziness of the others, created a vortex of energy in the exact center of the brothel. Along with these ghosts, there were two adult males, two children, and several female ghosts. The one female seemed to be very young and still resigned to her way of life. Enough so, that even in death she was still hitting-on men. At least one of the men in our group said he was being touched inappropriately!

A good friend of mine was running the investigation. He took all eight of us to each of the rooms, and explained who had lived and worked within. In almost every room, our meters lit up to let us know there could possibly be someone around. Things were active, I could feel the energy building. At that point, a male voice was heard by several of us. There were also a few of us that saw a ghost cat, and sadly, the spirit of a young girl. It was the same young female I had sensed earlier. There was a chair out in the hall by one of the doors into a room, I knew she was sitting on it. An EMF detector that had been placed on the chair had gone-off several times—as if to answer questions that had been asked. I heard one of the others say, "Well, the chair is empty. Look underneath, it must be rigged." Others did, just to appease that person, but there was nothing there. At that point, the girl spirit must have vacated the chair and started making passes at my friend leading the group. It was pretty funny!

That same friend of mine is an expert with spirit boxes. He led us to one of the larger rooms so we could conduct a session with one. With all of us assembled in one tiny room, the energy level shot-up. He turned-on the spirit box, and immediately there was an overwhelming amount of spirit voices that came through on the box.

I heard the name Stephen come through. It hit me as funny because it was my recently passed father's name, and the spirit's voice sounded like his. I heard it again—the name Stephen—and knew without a doubt, it was my dad. I did not say anything, I had no proof. Then several people said, at the same time, "We heard, Exie!" Then the name Susie, my dad called me that, but these people would not know that. Then I heard Bruce; that's my maiden name.

I had tears in my eyes, they started to roll down my cheeks. My mom, who was seated in a chair next to me, snapped her head up to look at me. I could not speak, I simply shook my head in a yes motion to her. The shocked look on her face was sweet. She said to the group, "That's my husband."

My friend running the session looked right at me, a bit shocked himself. I told him, "Yes, that was my dad!"

Then my dad's voice, again, over the box, "Can't stay long."

I knew this was him, it was his voice, there was no question to me or my mom. His clues (all the names) were spot-on. He must have worked hard to get through to us over all the other spirits. I was so proud of him, and beyond touched by his action for my mom and me. Thank you Dad.

Coming out of my own shock, I looked around the room at the others standing facing us. Their expressions were that of pure shock after what had just happened. I asked who had heard Susie. I explained the meaning of that name, and of Bruce.

Just before the wonderful words came through from my father, I had been talking with my spirit guide. I was asking if she would please have one of the spirits coming through on the box say my name—mostly as a poke at my two investigation teammates in the room! My name is quite often the one spoken at investigations, and it has become a running joke between us. The respond I got for my spirit guide was a shock, she said, "I cannot reach them." We concluded the session, and moved to another room. I never had the chance to ask why she could not reach them.

I remembered several days after we returned home, and I asked my spirit guide then, "What did you mean the other day when you said you could not reach the spirits who were communicating through the box?"

Through telepathy she told me, "The reason I could not reach the ghosts in the building, nor the spirits coming through the box, they were all on different vibrational levels, different from mine."

Never in my wildest thoughts of ghosts and spirits, did I think she would deliver that message. With some knowledge of vibrational levels—different levels for different types of entities —but never considered they could not communicate between them. I should have, she is an angel, so she vibrates at higher levels than an earthbound ghost. Even the spirits and ghosts coming through the box were on different planes. A spirit that has gone home is on a higher level than that of an earthbound ghost, but not as high as a guardian angel. Not all angels are on the same vibrational plane either, it has to do with their evolution and level of learning. Discussion for a different chapter... or possibly a different book!

If you have an opportunity to do a ghost investigation aboard a ship, do it! The ship we investigated was the USS Edson, moored in the Saginaw River, in Bay City, Michigan.

Keep in mind the prevailing theory, that being on, or near the water, adds-to or heightens energy. Our expectation was the activity here would be high.

We booked a private investigation several months ahead of time. I have been on public investigations before, and they are a great way to start. I now prefer to go on private investigations, simply because the number of investigators, and skill level, is determined by you. This time, there would only be ten people on the entire ship. Perfect!

The first bit of amazement was when we pulled up to where she was moored. We had not expected her to be gigantic. I guess I missed the part where they referred to her as a destroyer! It was fun watching the others pull their cars into the parking lot with the same shocked look on their faces. All of us were chomping-at-the-bit to get the investigation started. They first had a safety-talk to deliver, there were some dangerous areas of which we needed to be aware. Then they talked about the service record of the Edson, which was very interesting information that can be useful during the investigation.

The discussion then moved on to the kinds of activity you might have on board the ship. Myself and another medium walked away at this point—we both like to go in blind, without information. My reasoning is, I think it lends credence to both the location and myself. Honestly, for me, it is more fun to bring up events up as they are happening, and watch the others' faces! Then I usually comment, "I take it this is an activity that they talked about?"

On board the ship, we used the mess area as a central spot for the staging area, and a meeting spot. It worked well because it was one of the only areas that the lights were being left on. One last reminder from the hosting paranormal team about carrying equipment vertical stairs on a ship, then they left us to our own devices. Gathering our investigative tools, we headed for the bowels of the ship, two flights down. Ready or not here we come was all I could think.

Traversing the ship, realizing the literal meaning of vertical on the stairs, we moved slow, ending our journey in some sort of engine room. Not sure what these engines were for, too small to be what drove this beast. This whole area was only accessible by walking single file on a catwalk. Seeming like a good place, we began our first EVP session.

The first few questions were the typical, "Is anyone here?" Then someone asked, "How did you die?" That's when it became real to me, in a totally different way. My dad had been a sailor. I felt for the men, for their families. Coming out my reverie I asked, "What was this area for? I thought we might get an EVP out of that, since a woman asked! Nothing audible, but we would have to wait and see if anything was caught on the recorders. Another question was asked, "Did you always work in this area?" There was an immediate reply from midair, "I did."

Around the corner from this area was the head, seaman term for bathroom. We were surprised it was there, but soon learned they tucked rooms, bunks and lockers everywhere and anywhere they could. In this area, the question, "Are you taking a shower?" was asked very tongue-in-cheek.

On my recorder, I would later discover there was an answer in a male voice. "Max, you taking a shower?" followed by, "You, Ray?" Getting this much active, intelligent conversation made me think I needed a second recorder for instant playback after questions are asked. In this situation, I know I would have stayed longer to see if I could have received more responses.

That was about the time I started having personal experiences. My hair was being played with, and I also had picked up a follower. I knew there was a male spirit right behind me—all the time. I kept this to myself for a while, until I knew for sure it was not the effects of being in such tight quarters. Once we moved into an area with more room around us, and overhead, my hair got touched again. I decided that was enough verification and said something to the group. I told them what had been going on, "Someone keeps touching my hair, playing with it. Plus, there is a male following me, it's a bit annoying, frankly!" When the group stopped laughing, they told me those were both claims of happenings on the ship, but only to one particular woman in a group. This is exactly why I do not want to know ahead of time what has happened in locations.

We moved aft, toward the back of the ship, or the stern, and stayed on the same level. The spirit activity picked up in intensity. In an area of mostly bunkbeds (births) for crewmen, we all spread out in what seemed like row after row of bunks. You would go insane in these births if you had any level of claustrophobia

Behind me I heard some conversation, not usual for me. I stopped, turned around, and back-tracked toward what seemed to be three to four murmuring voices. I walked up on four investigators—they were all standing together facing what looked like a tiny closet. Joining them, I could see three officers' jackets, hung up with a bit of perfect separation between them. The only difference was the one in the middle vigorously swinging back-and-forth. There was no air moving, that was not the cause. I walked in front of the closet several times to see if movement would make it swing. It is a steel ship (that was not going to be the cause) but I wanted to say I looked at everything. The ship had not swayed due to a passing ship. Even if it had, our judgement call was that all three jackets would have started to move. I even went back the next day to check for earthquake activity in the area—there had been none. All the jackets were on the same sort of hanger, and all the hangers were over the rod the same way. Then, the jacket slowed its movement, and was still like the others. We asked spirit if this was paranormal, and could they please do it again. It did not happen again. When I played back my recorder the next day, there was nothing—no otherworldly comments as I had hoped. Come to find out, no one caught any evidence on a recorder during this time. Even though one of the group actually witnessed the hanger dip down—like someone had pushed it—just before it started to swing. She was the only one to see it, and there was no video. We cannot call this paranormal (it is an anomaly) we chose to think we needed more proof. Maybe if it happened again?

Moving further aft, to the stern of the ship, to the location where a broken-hearted sailor took his own life. As was told to the group, he locked himself in a small area, and suffocated—just after he received a Dear John letter from his girl back home. We stopped just outside the room, where there seemed to be a conversation taking place that we could hear. None of us were talking, and a couple of us checked around to make sure we were indeed alone on the ship—we were. It was a conversation between two men. On my recorder, I picked up "We've been watching them," and there was a reply, but it was inaudible.

The conversation came to an abrupt halt. We all had been standing there silently, looking around the room, trying to catch a glimpse of a spirit, while the conversation was happening. The conversation ended, but we stayed and asked a few more questions, to see if we could get them talking again. Nothing came of it—at the time—and there was nothing on the recorders.

Only steps away, we entered the room with the hatch in the floor—where a sailor committed suicide—we all huddled in there. The energy in the room, likewise down in the hatch, was very low. My senses picked up a male, but it was very faint. My recorder did not get anything from here either.

Stepping out of that room, and over a bulkhead, I immediately turned right to enter the woodworking shop—

then stopped dead in my tracks. An unseen hand ran down my hair, on the right side of my head, from the crown to my neck. Right about then, I was over being touched, "Enough. That is enough touching of the hair. This is out of bounds, no more." Continuing on into the shop, there were three investigators standing there, staring at me. All with questioning looks on their faces. I explained, they razzed me; we all chuckled and moved on. Sadly, there were no EVP's on the recorder from the event.

We all requested a break at this point and headed back up to the mess to put stuff down, and then off the ship for a restroom stop. The fresh air, and time away from my stalker, was lovely!

Back on board we decided to stay topside and tour the deck. This ship saw action, so we thought there might be spirit energy left out here as well. There was no EVP fluctuation for us, so we headed back inside. We collected our gear and headed fore, the bow of the ship; I wanted to see the bridge.

The bridge was very cool. You could feel the power of the location, the nervous tension, and the residual energy of having to be ready for whatever may happen. We moved next to the officers' mess/war room area, all taking seats at the conference table. We ran an EVP session, with some role play mixed-in, the ladies took on the persona of bad girls that had been snuck on board. We asked if anyone wanted to play, so-to-speak!

While this was happening, some pictures and paperwork scattered on the table caught my attention. Glancing at a few of the pictures, and then for some reason looking up at a picture on the wall, I got the name Roy. I was not sure why, but thought perhaps he was coming forward and was ready to play. That thought did not thrill me, but we did start it. Telling the group the name Roy, we asked a few questions, and the energy in the room went totally flat. Something had happened to change that, but we were not sure what. I mentioned, perhaps all he wanted was for us to know his name.

From here, we noticed steps and took those down one level. As it turns out, we found what is known as the 9/11 room. Immediately following the attacks on 9/11 in New York, all across the country, communication rooms like this were set up in different locations. This room on the Edson was one of those rooms.

We passed through this room for the time being; we would return, and be glad we did. Entering what looked to be a hall loaded with births, straight ahead was the bow of the ship. This area had 2 small rooms, no windows, and not a breath of moving air. We shut the bulkhead door and turned off all flashlights; it was dead silent and dead still. I was sensing spirit energy, but not fresh energy. It felt as if what had been in here, vacated when we came in. Having had enough of the confined space that was getting hotter by the minute, we pushed open the door, which gave us a view straight down the hall, past the births. There, to our delight, were several shadow people peeking around the beds looking in our direction. We could perfectly make out their heads and shoulders. They did not stay visible long; in a heartbeat they rapidly pulled backward from our view.

Leaving that room, we moved forward a few steps, turning left past several rows of births on both sides. We found the peeking shadow people among the beds. This aisle deadened up ahead of us into a birth. If you turned left, it was a dead end, but to the right, it led you right back into the 9/11 room. I paused in the dead end row to run an EVP session. I knew we were surrounded, but wanted them to come out and interact with us. We kept seeing them peek at us, down toward the entrance to the 9/11 room, but that was all we were getting. While we were in this area, I heard the strangest noise, a high-pitched squeak, female, totally out-of-place—my recorder would back me up. I caught that high-pitched squeak and more. During the playback on my recorder, I caught a female voice. At the time you could not tell what she said, however on playback with my headset on, I could. The squeak came first, and then to my utter surprise, she said, "Help me."

Later, in the 9/11 room, we circled-up to run an EVP session with some of our REM Pod and EMF detectors. This was a large room, with a few tables and file cabinets. Perfect! We could face each other and see behind each other at the same time. The REM Pod was placed in the entry way at the other end of the room. Pretty much, all of us held an EMF detector out in front of ourselves—one lit up a green dot—that was fast, and a tease, as far as I was concerned. We did not get too excited, outwardly anyway! They were asked to come forward, to light up more of the detectors, or simply more lights on that one. It lit up one more of the dots past the green, then the next one. That detector stayed in the red, but then several other detectors lit up simultaneously. It seems we had attracted a group. We suspected it was the shadow people that we spotted in the hall. This was an intelligent haunt—they were doing exactly as we asked.

Off to my left, in my peripheral vision, I spotted movement. This would be back in the hallway of births that we passed to get into this room. Apparently, we did not have all the shadow people with us in the circle. The other medium and I glanced at each other and smiled; he had noticed it on his right side. Just then, the REM Pod started to sing its awful song and scared the crap out of all of us. We had been lost in the moment with our shadow people, in the circle and the hallway. This activity showed us that there were at least four to five spirits with us simultaneously.

Someone thought it a good idea to use a laser grid down the hall to my left. That was great with me; I had never used one during an investigation. With the grid set-up, and the EMF detectors still lighting up on command, my friend, and team member, standing to my right, started an EVP session. Each of the first few questions were answered immediately, by utilizing the lights on her EMF detector. Then things changed, and she got more than she bargained for. It seemed, to us, that one of the sailor spirits had taken-a-liking to her. He must have liked long hair, or just her ponytail, but he kept touching it. He would light up the detector in response to her question while touching her hair. I gave her a lot of credit for just standing there while this was happening! Meanwhile, the spirit in the hall to my left was starting to work his way down toward us. With that happening, I looked down at my detector and it was completely lit up—they all were. With heart-stopping effect, someone sneezed and all activity stopped. It never came back to what it was for those few moments, as hard as we tried. We packed our gear and headed up to the mess, we all needed some fresh air.

Working our way along halls, upstairs, and into the final hall, I could hear voices ahead of me, I assumed in the mess area. Closer to the mess, I could see the room was empty. Then it hit me! I spun around, and headed back toward the empty office that I had just passed. The voices I had heard must have been coming from there. Arriving at the office doorway, one person was outside and two were just inside. The conversation was still going on; we stood in silence. Peeking into the office, there was a chair at the far end of the room, I knew someone had just been sitting in it. At this point, I sidestepped approximately a foot into the room. I needed to feel activity as it was happening. Turning to look back at the people standing in the doorway, I whispered, "Does it feel, to you, like someone one was just here, in particular, in that chair?" One woman shook her head yes. I continued… "I wonder where they went?" My recorder gave me the answer.

Later, when I played this part back on the recorder, I shot-off the couch like I had been electrocuted, making a loud whoop sound; scared my husband and my dog half to death! "Sorry guys!"

There was a reply to my question of, "I wonder where they went?" In an intimate whisper, near my right ear, a male voice said, "Right behind you!"

To date, this is the best Class A EVP I have ever capture; it was a direct answer to a question! I will certainly never forget this moment.

With all thoughts of a break forgotten, we moved next to an area referred to as Paul's room. It is a large area that now only has two bunks in it; I would assume at one point there were more. On one wall, there was a huge closet/storage area, filled with era-specific seaman clothing. As the hours ticked by, we were starting to get tired and a bit silly. Getting our act together, somewhat, we started an EVP session. One of the questions posed was if the bunk had bed bugs? We chuckled. On my recorder, I had a male voice say, "Bed bugs?" More questions about who stayed in this room… was it really a Paul? The next question, I thought a good one, asked if there were ever women on board this ship? My recorder picked up a word, in a female voice, right after the question from a woman on board: "Mine!" Not sure what she was referring to. The reply was right after the question, but the answer did not fit for me. After her reply came a deep sigh close to the microphone on the recorder. Then, there was a weird noise—I could not tell if it was just noise or words.

Feeling done in there, we filed-out and said goodbye as we did. My recorder also picked up a male voice yelling, "Hey!" while we were all in the hall, just outside Paul's room. It was not heard at the time.

Very few of the voices and sounds caught on my digital recorder were heard at the time they happened. I feel it is a very important part of my investigation equipment. It lends credence to things I am feeling at the time, but do not hear.

###

Chapter 4

Love Never Dies

Loss is hard, no other way to say it. It is also a reality of life. The old saying goes "no one gets out alive!" is a fact we would rather, and try our damnedest to, ignore. I have had much death in my lifetime. I was born into a family with many older generations in, it was hard—too many of them died when I was twelve and thirteen years of age. This collided with my personal life, I was physically changing—and had started seeing dead people.

Those deaths confused me; I felt lost and hurt for many years after there passings. One person in my world understood me, my Aunt. She talked me through much of the confusion, more accurately, she listened well. I was not equipped to deal with this much loss and the grief. I was trying to come to terms with the feeling of being left behind… that feeling created a question: left behind from what? I did not know at this age that there was more; were my past life memories coming through? Stuffing these and more questions away,. I would wait many years for answers.

Present life, the year is 2016. Much water has passed under the bridge, but I still miss so many of those people that died when I was a child. My heart no longer hurts for them—my heart is now warmed by them—a welcomed change of feeling. I now try to help others with the passing of their family and friends. I guess my childhood was the primer for this, it was hard, but if I can help, then I am thankful for the years in the past.

It was the middle of the night, early morning to some, 2:31 a.m. I was awoken with the sensation that something or someone was coming. I laid there and waited. It was not long before a spirit blasted through my bedroom window. He zoomed across the room and hovered over me, staring me in the face. He was a young male, too young to be in spirit. My heart broke, there would be distraught family and friends waking up to bad news shortly.

He was very upset; this was a surprise to me. I guess I assumed, since he had done this to himself, he would not be so upset. Immediately, it crossed my mind that I knew he had done this to himself, that knowing was new. Telepathically, he said to me, "Tell her I loved her." I knew, too, this was unrequited, she thought him a dear friend, but not a lover.

I said back, "I will figure out a way to deliver your message."

Having said that, my eyes closed and I went back to sleep. I assumed he would move on to the next person on his visitation list, but no. I woke up again (it was still dark out); I checked the time—it was 3:31 a.m. Rolling on my back, I looked up, right into the face of the young man, he was still there. I was shocked that he had stayed. I told him then, "I am going back to sleep. I will deliver the message, but not for many hours. You need to leave." He left, but came back when I got into my car at 8 a.m. to go workout. He was in the backseat. An old song, with lots of meaning, came on the radio. I knew it was from him. He knew I was headed to the location that I could possibly deliver the message.

I did deliver the message to a person, and she promised to tell the person to which he had been referring. I honestly was not sure if it would happen or not. The feeling coming from this person, and the look on her face, was skeptical. I knew she would think this over, and do what she thought was best at the time. I had done all I could do.

I received a text later in the day that said, "Message delivered —the information is being digested." That was all that was ever said by any of us.

He never came back. I assume he was good with everything. God Bless you, young man.

###

Dear Loved Friend,

I will remember you always. I will miss you until the day we meet again. I will love you always. Thank you for teaching me what love is on a Universal level.

In the car on the last leg of our drive to Florida, my husband and I had literally just pulled onto the freeway in the southern part of North Carolina. My fourth tiny cup of coffee was just kicking in, we were excited to see family later in the day, and we were happy. After all, this was the beginning of the next chapter of our life.

In the car's center counsel, my phone rang. We looked at each other, it was 7:30 a.m.—not good—too early for the phone to ring. I picked the phone up to see the readout, but it did not list a contact name. It listed a state of origination for the call, that was all. It rang and rang, it did not go to voice mail which was odd. I answered it.

The voice on the other end was vaguely familiar. It was hard to tell, his voice was raspy, he was crying and began talking rapidly. My husband gives me the hang it up look, but I knew not to hang up, but to let this play out. I gave him my chill, it is okay face!

It finally registered, it was my good friend's husband on the other end of the phone. He was trying to tell me my beloved friend had passed the night before. I went numb, this was the worst, most shocking news.

In shock, I realized that my husband had been asking me what is wrong. It was then I noticed that my hair was being pulled and played with. The message was really sent home when there was one good tug. Ouch!

That brought me back to the present. I looked at my husband with tears in my eyes, and whispered the news to him. He frowned deeply, whispering back, "I am sorry." Moments later, the called came to an end, he had others to contact.

I smiled, cried, laughed, and cursed as I told my husband what had been happening with my hair while I talked on the phone. He laughed and said he wondered why I said ouch. In my head, at this moment, I heard my friends voice, "Wow, woman! Notice me already!" That was so him, I started to sob.

This was a huge conflict of the heart for me. I was in a car with my husband, almost to Florida. How do I get to Ohio for the funeral that I should attend? There was only one person who could answer that. I asked my newly departed friend, "Will you be mad at me for not attending? It is simply not feasible for me to make it." I did not really think he would be mad at me, but in my sorrow, it came out that way.

The answer came to me in music, for three days. Each of those days, when I would get in the car, the first three to five songs that played were directed at me. The first two songs were the same every day. They were followed by songs that had a strong message that pertained to something that happened in our friendship. He and I had talked several times about messages in music, we both believe it happens. This then, was fitting; the hair pulling happened a couple more times and then ceased. On social media, I was reading that he had pulled the hair of many others—great verification.

I miss you, dear man, with every cell in my being. We will communicate often, I sure. I know that one day, when I return home, you will be there for me with open arms. The story does not end here.

Days later, I received an invitation to participate on an internet radio show honoring our friend. Of course, I said yes, and was thankful for being included.

Calling into the show was very emotional. Many callers talked, told stories, and some, too shook up, left heartfelt messages in the chat room. All of us were heartbroken and still in shock at his sudden, and much too soon, passing.

The clear message, from all these wonderful people, was that he was the personification of love. He was a seeker of the good and kind. He was a collector, like no other; items of which he adorned his home, and life. He hugged with purpose.

Thank you, buddy, for helping me keep the laughter in my life—and the love in my heart.

###

Chapter 5

A Medium is Brought to Life

My father taught me the value of friends and connections. In this life event, these friends have an internet radio show and invited me on. The female part of this duo helped me take the necessary steps toward my future.

I love these two people, they are a cute husband-wife duo, but are amazing separately. They have discovered a nice balance, with practice I am sure! Their show, like most of the others, is live. They had decided we should do readings and asked how I felt about it. I agreed and immediately regretted that decision. I had barely started doing face-to-face readings, let alone readings over the phone. Questions about my decision were plaguing me. How does this work? Would it work? I was terrified that I would embarrass myself.

I sent them a message full of unfounded fear. They assured me that they would take good care of me, and it would be fine. I was not convinced, but I did trust them.

My other concern, something out of my control, the callers' questions: I was assuming all their questions would be about relationships or money. At this point in my learning process, I was not being shown these things. Those questions about the future are for a psychic—mediums talk to dead people.

By the afternoon of the radio show, I felt sick to my stomach. I knew I was going to throw up. It was just nerves, but perfectionist, worry-wort Virgo was taking over!

At dinner, my husband had me eat some protein. He knew I would need it to be able to function. If I was going to do readings, I would need fuel to burn. He was right, so I ate a little and actually felt somewhat better.

Almost showtime, I asked for help from my spirit guide and settled in. I sat in a large leather chair off in a spare room, it was quiet. There was some lead-in items, then it was my turn. They introduced me and immediately started taking callers. Oh Lord! My stomach rolled, I thought they might hear the noise it made.

My first caller was a woman from South Carolina, "I want a man! When will he show up?" We all laughed, and then they tossed the question to me. What happened to the safety net? Not my area, or so I thought. I hemmed and hawed for a moment, buying some time to tune in to my spirit guide better. An image appeared, an image of a man. I gave her all the particulars about him, and when I thought they might meet. She was not a bit happy about the fact that it was going to be a long time before they met. I was then told that she already knows this guy. She started to argue with me, until I described the gentleman to a T. I was pleased when she admitted she did, indeed, already know him! That stopped her in her tracks. She told me she was shocked that I had received his description that well. I did not say it, but I agreed. She was please to know this, and we ended the call.

Next caller, same question and same result. "He is several months out for a meet-up timeframe. Do not get mad at me, that fact is not my doing or my fault! You must see that learning some patience is also a part of your path". For both women, these gentlemen were on the way, relax. I gave what I was given, that is all I can do.

My friend, the radio host, took the next two questions; I appreciated the break. The next caller had to be my favorite to-date—the fact she was calling from Hawaii helped. It was the reading that rocked my world, and built my confidence up to where it should have been. It began like the others, she also wanted relationship information. It was a little different because she wanted info on a man with which she was already in a relationship.

In my mind, I saw a hula dancer, a beautiful woman, she was outside on a beach. She was tan, long straight black hair, with traditional hula attire, a grass skirt and bikini top. In front of her, a tiger appeared. It was an older, Asian-art style tiger; it reminded me of Asian-art tattoos. My vision then drifted off to the right. I was being shown a tall stand of bamboo. None of this made sense to me. I learned from this reading not to judge what I was getting, but to tell the client everything I was being shown. It might mean the world to your client, so tell them.

I told her everything. She said she knew the woman, and the man—he has a tattoo of the tiger in that exact style, and the tiger is standing by bamboo.

Next I was being shown, in front of the tiger, a wrought iron cross in an old gothic style. I told her these images are past, present and future. I knew she and the man were headed toward a religious event. She told me yes, thank you. She continued, the hula woman is this man's ex-wife and she is gorgeous! The man with the tiger tattoo is her fiancée, and the iron cross is on the steeple of the church where the ceremony was being held. She had been unsure if they would make it to the church; things were getting bumpy for them.

The next caller wanted to know if there were any spirits in her house. In the time it took her to take a breath, to continue her question, the image of a man appeared before me. He quickly blanched away from me, I guess in an effort not to make eye contact, but he stayed there in profile. He had long, dark brown hair with a long bang combed over his forehead. He also had a thin mustache, often referred to as a pencil mustache. His clothing consisted of a button-down shirt, suspenders, and high-waisted trousers with a cuff at the hem. He had on leather lace-up shoes. He looked to be from the 1940s, and I picked up he had a massive ego!

This description meant nothing to her, but she admitted she did not know about all her ancestors. I told her he wants to be known; I got that from the way he came into the reading, quick and strong. I moved on from him, because his image was being replaced by that of an older couple, very sweet faces.

The gentleman that came in next was in overalls, and his wife was in a plain dress, with an apron over top. They let me know they were immigrants from Germany, and had come here to be free. Both had large strong bodies, with big wonderful smiles on their faces. This image, for me, seemed to be from the 1920s.

She was disappointed and expressed that fact: "Well, I don't know any of them, why are they in my house?" I had to chuckle, not out of rudeness (people assume they were the only ones to ever have been in a location) when in reality, that is far from the truth. There have been many that came before us.

I told her, "They lived in the house first. It is an old house, on old land. I am shocked they are the only ones living there!"

She said, "WHAT?" This time, I laughed heartily!

Our next caller was, once again, questioning when she would find love. My answer was not well-received. I told her early in 2017 (she wanted a man by Christmas 2016) which was only a month away! I saw a large, white tent, like the kind people rent for events or ceremonies. The sides were all open, it was nice weather, the grass was green, and the trees all had leaves. This type of weather, where she was from—the eastern seaboard, is late June time frame.

Under the tent, seated at a table for eight, sat a man—alone. He was casually seated in the chair, not in a rush or impatiently waiting, just waiting. What I picked up from this was he was waiting for her, and I told her that. She was a bit happier with that news. She wanted to know what he was wearing... he had on a nice suit, a thin gray pinstripe, expensive looking. Still insistent, she said, "No, he needs to arrive in cold weather."

I told her, "Someone might, but not the right someone. You need to relax, and attend every event you are invited to, he is waiting—just like you are."

"What does he look like?"

I was not completely sure, spirit would not show me his face. In fact, they would not show him above the shoulders. I could tell he had a nice build, lean, like a runner's build. He was seated, so I could not even tell his approximate height. He was watching everything that was going on under the tent—he was looking for her.

Our only male caller for the evening had psychic abilities of his own; we all picked up on those right away. He was looking for reassurance of those abilities. His father was coming in, for me to let him know he was proud of him, and to tell him he loves him.

I am often a bit leery of people with this much ability. I find all they want is their ego stroked, and I had no time for that. We were short on time, and wanted to get as many caller questions as possible. He turned out to be a very nice guy, so did his dad.

After the show was over, I had a massive adrenaline rush, and did not get to sleep until the early morning hours. Phone readings are much better for me now, I use my energy wisely—I have learned to use my spirit guides' energy instead of mine.

I have heard mediums and psychics talk about the shorthand they have with their spirit guides; I finally understand what they mean. By shorthand, you could also say shortcut. My spirit guide and I create more of a shorthand every time we connect. It seems she shows me something new each time; this is a great tool! It is not always obvious what spirit is trying to get across, especially without the use of spoken communication. I mostly see images clairvoyantly. I am evolving, I do now hear certain words from spirits. People that hear messages are called clairaudient.

As an example of shorthand, and how I am shown things, this reading is a perfect example. I had been talking with my client, conducting a phone reading, and our time was almost up. A young man of about thirty-eight years of age came into the reading. He stood right next to the woman's paternal grandfather, who had come in earlier. I thought that there was a connection to them, possibly his brother, that is my shorthand on that. Usually, relations stand by each other. Thinking it was an uncle, I started to describe him. While I was describing him, his image, at least my vision of him, kept evolving. He was handsome, with short, brown hair, and had on a dark blue suit.

As I was describing the suit, his image started to rotate clockwise away from me. When he rotated around, what should have been the back of his head with hair, was not hair—it was the exact image of his face on the other side of his head. I sincerely had no idea what this was about or what to say. The thought that came to mind first, was that he was two-faced. Did this pertain to his personality? Was he an ass? Did this have to do with his mental state? Was he bipolar?

I asked my client if any of this made sense. Did you have an uncle on your dad's side with mental issues? Perchance, did he work in a job that was secret, or had covert operations involved with it? Something like the CIA? I was trying to fill-in where I was being left off, information-wise, from my spirit guide. She said, "I'm not sure, and have no idea what he did for a living… seems odd that I don't know." She told me she would ask her mom later.

Hours later that day, I got a private message on social media from her. She asked if this guy could possibly have been an ex-boyfriend; he had passed away a few years ago. I inquired about his hair color, age, and a couple of other things and it did fit. Then she said, "Oh, and he was an identical twin!" My mind was blown! Twins had never crossed my mind! I have never brought in twins. Plus, let's be honest, that was a tough read. I think there must be a better shorthand to represent twins. Another thing that threw me off, was where he came into the reading—usually that is a spot representative of a close family member, not someone outside the circle of family. She could explain that as well. He was amazingly close to her grandfather in life. There you have it, the spirit tried to connect to him for her. Of course, it would not mean anything to me, but I told her about it—and in the long run it helped.

She told me that in the hours since we had spoken, this was all she could think about. I am incredibly glad she could sort it out. I am also glad she was understanding of the situation.

I booked my first-ever event, referred to as a Medium Party! I had a fabulous time meeting all the women I read, and their families. I love that I get to help people reconnect and find peace. Thank you.

This event came about when I met a woman at a book event. She was vivacious, and a very talented artist. She asked me many questions, and I did the same, about her craft. We exchanged contact information, and I honestly thought that was that.

Many months later, my phone rang and it was this woman. She wanted me to come do a reading party at her friend's house. She had seven vendors and eighty women coming to the event! She asked me if this would work for me? I laughed, "Hell yes, this works." I told her that was way too many people for me to read in the allotted time, so I would invite some other mediums to join us. Date and time were set, address was given, and we were on. Immediately, I contacted two other mediums and a numerologist to work with me.

I had never done readings in this manor, meaning back-to-back for two-and-a-half hours straight. I had a few concerns; the biggest, that I might disappoint someone due to exhaustion. I needed to learn to trust. I will have to get what I need, when I need it.

I thought this might be a good event for my mom to attend (a long afternoon) perfect to get her out of the condo. The event location was a forty-five minute drive from the house, but went by fast conversing with my mom. I let her know what to expect from the event, at least what I expected. With four mediums, the energy can become intense in a closed-up house. Little did I know, this was not going to be a problem!

Pulling in the driveway, we drove for almost ten minutes

before we even saw the house. It was a magnificent seven thousand square foot log home, no confined, closed-in issues at this house.

Greeted at the door, we were given a complete tour; the place was three stories of magnificence. I selected a spare bedroom on the third floor over a suspended walkway—it suited my mood. We met the vendors, and some early guests, all very sweet people. I set my mom up at the ten-person kitchen island, and went up stairs to start doing readings.

The other mediums were getting ready to start as well, that made me happy. I would not see the other mediums for the next two-and-a-half hours!

As the first people were walking up the stairs for readings with us, we conducted a blessing on the event. That made the energy feel right, so we could begin.

My first client sat down, who was the homeowner, as I began talking to my spirit guide. "I know I am ready for this day, or you would not have brought me to it. Please help me strongly connect with you, so I can get wonderful and true messages for all that come to me. Thank you."

The homeowner, whom I had never met, was a sweet, easy-going woman. Her deceased family came rushing in to speak with her, it was touching. I felt great after her reading, things had gone smoothly and I was strong. When she opened the door to leave, women were lined-up outside the door waiting. I was excited, proud, and shocked! My spirit guide scolded me for the shocked part. I am learning to trust the strong medium that I am, it is all good.

Person after person came and went in twenty minute increments. They were all delightful and very trusting… I learned a valuable lesson from that. They are trusting me to be honest and true. Be who they expect, and life will be amazing. I gave them every bit of information I was receiving from spirits. Some was shocking, some was confusing, and some information made them cry. I gave them what they came for. I was impressed with spirit for their magnificence on this day. That was a fun afternoon.

My last client left the room, I packed the few things I brought for my table, and joined the few people remaining down stairs. My mom and I said thank you to the woman who set this up, and the homeowner for hosting. As my mom and I were stepping through the massive front door onto the front porch, there was a whisper in my ear: "Thank you!"

Startled, I turned to see if there was someone standing close enough to have said this, there was not. My heart had never been so touched by a message. Just as the door was shutting, I said, "You are welcome. Happy I could be here. Thank you!"

I learned many things from this experience. First, to trust my spirit guide, she has my back. Also, to trust myself, and my gift. Spirit gave me correct, poignant, heartfelt messages for the waiting loved ones sitting in front of me.

My world has changed immensely in the last five years. I was told by a psychic, years ago that in this time frame I would look back at my life and not recognize it. I admit I questioned that, but she was absolutely correct. I know, too, there are more additions to my gifts on the way... something develops almost daily.

It was an honor and a pleasure to read for a friend's mother. This beautiful woman was grieving badly, and needed some peace. I do not take money for these types of readings, it goes against everything inside of me. My understanding of grief of this nature is close-to-home.

I called the daughter's phone and was placed on speaker, so both mother and daughter could hear. Several spirits immediately came through. However, my spirit guide stepped-in and made them wait. She then show me a beautiful rose bush, covered with pink and red blooms. There were hearts floating up from the top of the bush. This was being shown to express all the love from the universe, from her past ancestors, and her dearly departed husband.

The moment I was done explaining, the ancestors were allowed back in. There was a grandparent, a great grandparent, an uncle, and finally her husband appeared. I knew this was the spirit with which she really wanted to communicate, her daughter had told me. We made the others wait, again, and talked to him.

He sent more love and asked her to please not be sad. He wanted her to find a grief group. She started to cry. He asked her not to be alone, he wanted her to get out of the house, find friends, do things—to live the life that she was ignoring now. He said this is what she would want of him. Then, he had to go, but made sure she understood he would always be close.

She told me that this helped her feel more at peace; I cannot ask for more than that from a reading. I, too, was relieved, for them both. Her daughter spoke-up and said she felt it, too. I was smiling from ear to ear.

As a medium, I have been given these abilities to help. If I can help someone get to a peaceful place in their life, my heart wells with happiness on that fact alone.

Thank you, spirit guides, for the fabulous messages you brought out way and helped me deliver. Thank you, also, to the other family members that came through and were so patient with us. They had wonderful messages of love to deliver as well.

###

Once again, I was headed back to my childhood home. This excites me more than I can express in words. However, this time I was going back to do a reading for the homeowner. She also requested help with (possibly) identifying the spirit in the house that watches her. I had always felt someone watching me in the house, from the exact same area, the dining room. Interesting and affirming that someone else was feeling this. I thought I had figured out that it was the spirit of my great uncle—the one who is attached to a photo, and residing at my current home in the garage.

As I entered the house, a ball of light appeared, midair, in the center of the living room. It rapidly traveled forward about three feet and disappeared. Simultaneously, we were being watched by a second sprit, the one in the dining room. Ahh, to be home! It struck me as weird that the spirit in the dining room would look so much like my great uncle, but not be him —I had no idea who he was.

We sat in arm chairs in the living room, there was a small table between us. Conversation with her is so easy and upbeat. We talked of life, work, and family. She is truly a talented painter and a yoga master. We discussed her work for a while, then touched on, artistically, the new path she was on. Spirit was pushing me to begin the reading, so we did.

Being seated in this room brought back a lifetime of memories. Christmases, birthdays, and simply hanging out with my parents and siblings. Heartwarming times mostly, but a few tough times tossed into the mix, as any family, I suppose.

The reading was good, not easy by any means, but good. She is already spiritually connected, so many times spirits see no sense in coming in at the time of the reading. They feel as if they are communicating with her all the time already. With the reading done, I turned outward, into the house to see what I could pull in there. I felt the young boy spirit from my childhood. He was on the third step from the top of the basement stairs. He was nosey and listening intently to our conversation. I could feel his emotions change, as it dawned on him just who I was. This was getting exciting, it had been twenty-eight years since he would have seen me last. I smiled, wondering if he thought I looked old now!

Turning away from him, I focused on the male spirit in the dining room, per request. He was tall, dark-haired— the same as my great uncle, but I knew this was not him. Tuning in to him more, I tried to pull him in closer. To no avail, he was revealing nothing more to me. I did have the faintest feeling that he might have something he wished to say to the homeowner. I got another feeling that the message was not directly for her, instead for her to relate to someone. Frustratingly, that was all I could pull in, then he shut down. I relayed this to the homeowner, she thought it interesting, but confusing, as did I.

We ended my visit, and I headed to my car. When I arrived earlier, I parked, in my old spot on the curb, right in front of the house. Getting back into my car, my attention was sharply drawn to a set of windows on the front of the house, to the left. That was my parents' old bedroom. The spirit of the little boy was splayed against the glass of the windows saying goodbye to me. He was smiling and waving like crazy, so I waved back. He had indeed figured out who I was. In my head, I heard, "I thought it was you. Hi! I did recognize you."

A happy tear, for all the terrifying years of my childhood, escaped and slid down my cheek. All the tough, yet wonderful, years in this house rushed back to me—in an instant.

Pulling my gaze from the little boy in the window, I put the car in Drive and pulled away. Steeped in memories all the way home, I could hardly wait to share all this with my guys.

It is true, you can never go home to plant. You can, however, go home to fill back up with the memories of all that helped make you who you are today. This day was one of the greatest gifts of my life.

###

Once the path to mediumship fully opened for me, my life completely changed. An unbelievable number of doors have opened, and I am grateful. I have been conducting several readings a week, and booking large group readings as well. The learning curve has been steep at times, with events unfolding so rapidly. This is not a complaint; it has been wonderful and wondrous, simultaneously. Part of the curve is getting comfortable with a new path, and all the parts associated with what that path brings. I am dealing with peoples' lives—much care, love, and respect must be shown at every turn. There is no room for ego on this path. Confidence, yes; that helps my readings be stronger. I thought that my life was complete when I wrote my first book and took it on the road. I know now, that was only the beginning; I could not be happier about it either.

My mediumship has helped to round me out, and to ease my mind. It has brought a clarity, that I have been a medium my whole life; that is where the ease comes in. Knowing that fact, now eases my mind about all the things I have known my entire life—things I could not know—things about people, feelings, and situations.

I understand that I have years of learning yet to come. One night, not long ago, I had a drear I was walking toward a ladder, stepped upon the first rung and knew it was right. It felt good, I was supposed to be there. Holding firmly onto the rung above, with both hands, I took another step up. Glancing up the ladder, it continued up into the sky, through the clouds, and out of sight. The clouds parted, enough to see shards of light from the sun bursting through; it felt comfortable. It showed me that I will be welcoming a new way of life. Without a doubt, this was the metaphor of my life-path. Keep taking those steps, keep learning, keep trying, it is all waiting for you.

###

Exie Susanne Smith

Chapter 6

New Abilities

It has been about two years now, that I realized I have the ability to look at a photo and tell what is going on. With photos of people, I am very accurate in knowing if they are dead or alive. In photos of dwellings, I can tell if it is haunted, and if so by whom.

I have been contacted several times by families, and friends of these families, to see if I can help them find a missing person. Because of the extremely delicate nature of these events, I will keep the retelling to my experiences only.

Life has been wonderful, normal highs and lows, but less turmoil and that is a good thing. Relaxing on the couch, no rush to do anything, I opened social media. I noticed there was a private message waiting for me. The note was from a woman with whom I went to high school. She lives in different state, but still in the Midwest.

Her note to me described a situation where a young man was missing. There was some family history of depression and suicide—needless to say the family was terrified. Writing back to her, I informed her that I had never worked on a missing person case, but would do whatever I could to help.

Asking my spirit guide for assistance and guidance was the first step I took, trying to bring him in, to visualize him. I sat back in my quiet home and concentrated on him. In my mind, I was being shown a wooded area, a path, then a person—an extremely distraught person. I could not see his face, there was a hood in the way; he was wearing a hoodie. With time, I learn my spirit guide shielded his face from me, she told me it was for my protection. She knew I was too new at this, and my emotions would become over-invested. I was told, by her, that she did not want me looking into his eyes. She knew it would break my heart, and possibly derail me from the path I needed to be on.

I saw several other images involving this person, but not if he was dead or alive. I saw the car he had driven to this location, and again the path he walked to get to the secluded spot where he seated. I also saw a house on a small rise. The house was pink and had a circular driveway, and a hedge out front. I relayed all of this to my friend. She was going to pass the information along to the family.

Over the next several months, I tuned in to this person, and the feeling I got, was that he was fine. I was correct—in a way. He was fine because he was home. I find out he had done himself harm, and was in heaven with other family members. I was picking him up with family, and sadly, I had the wrong location of where all this took place.

I was shattered for the family. I cried, off and on, for many days, stopping to pray for him, and them. He was so young and confused; I felt sad to the bone for all of them. I went back to my roots and talked to the God that I know, asking him questions. I had never believed that suicide kept you from heaven. Surely, God would not turn someone away that was in such despair, so confused. My spirit guide told me to use my abilities and tune in to this young man, which I did. I found him in heaven; whole, healed, happy, and learning about the life he had just left behind. I was relieved.

In this new world as a medium, I am feeling, seeing, and closely interacting with death. It has taught me what a joyous reunion it is with our higher powers, spirits, families, friends, and past pets.

A second high school friend contacted me, thank the Lord, not with a missing person case. Again, this was for a friend, but this time, about a job situation. This thing, that was happening at work, was bad for her. She wanted to quit, but could not. I was confused and asked my spirit guide for clarity, or an out!

I was told by the woman's spirit guide that she was being

coerced. I was told by my friend it was because she is at the top of her pay scale. Her gut was telling her that her boss wanted her gone because of the high salary. She felt betrayed and hurt; she has given her all at this job. She had been job hunting, but nothing has come of it. I thought, at first, she needed to close one door, so another could open. After typing that, I typed something I consciously do not remember: "This job is physically affecting her heart, it is time to move on."

Looking down at my computer screen, waiting for her reply, I noticed that line of typing, and thought it was from her. It was with my response, I had typed that, and did not realize it. I had heard of automatic writing, but not automatic typing. Same premise, when you think about it.

I knew I was supposed to say that (to trust) so I was not worried about it. My friend was equally shocked, and replied, "YES, it is physically affecting her heart!" She was excited to tell her friend about our conversation. I hope it helped and that she had enough time at the job for a full retirement.

I have not inquired about her course of action, I was not sure it was my place to ask. If she wanted to me to know, she would have dropped me a note. I continue to wish her well.

I saw a picture on my social media feed, it was of a sweet baby laying on a blanket. To most of the respondents on the feed, the picture looked to them as the caption read, "A baby powder fart!" I had a feeling otherwise.

Instantly this picture spoke to me, it told me that it was a spirit hovering over the baby. I posted that in the feed, and seconds later she replied, "I knew it was more."

My senses picked up that it was one of the baby's grandmas; it was not being made clear which one though. She and I switched our messaging to private, where I described the woman I was seeing. "She has a sweet face, full cheeks, gray styled hair, short—she was funny in life, fun loving, and happy. She always seemed to have on an apron, and a smile. She is asking for your permission to come and stay around you and your daughter." The spirit then asked me to say the following: "If you say yes to this, when your daughter gets older, I will be playing with her in her room. When you hear her talking, it will only be me! We met before she was born, she will recognize me, we are old friends." I had to laugh at this; add strong-willed to the description list! Love is eternal and powerful.

She is one of the happiest spirits I have ever had the pleasure of meeting. Her excitement over the fact I could tell it was her, and communicate her wishes, was amazing to her. I told her, "Watch for her, she will be in the house."

She wanted clarification, "Watch for what?"

"I was told it would be cold spots, mists, dizzy feelings, and noises that are not typical to the house."

This was fabulous fun to share with her—and all from the comfort of my couch.

Later in the day, I received two pictures from this woman of her mother and grandmother. The one picture was exactly how this spirit presented herself to me, exactly!

Today was thrilling! I took a chance, commented on a photo out of the blue, and reunited three generations of women. It was a gift for us all.

This house has had an ongoing haunting, which we have been a part of, for at least five years. I have been here alone, or with as many as five others. This time coming to the house, I was not taking any chances, and brought six others with me: my investigation team, and a couple other investigative teams' members (it so happened that two of those people are mediums). We needed answers, and to try to find the bottom of this paranormal well.

As usual, when you pulled into the drive, you felt the spirits in the house looking out windows at you. They knew we were coming, and had been waiting for us to arrive. We gathered our tools and gadgets, said a prayer as a group, and headed to the door.

I have always known there was an older female spirit in the house. It is the male homeowner's mother. She has come to live with them since they had a baby. Actually, a fairly common event! She also let me know that she was there to protect them from the others; that creeped me out when she told me that. I had yet to pick up the other spirits in the house. I felt there was an older male in the house, he was new to me. When I first picked up on him, I thought it was the female homeowner's grandfather. We did eventually pick up on a grandfather, but up in the second floor loft. There was a chair in the area where we picked him up, and thought he might be attached to that. By the end of the investigation, I did not think that anymore. He was merely sitting in the chair and had taken-a-liking to it.

In the basement of the house, we picked up an older man. Someone in the group felt that there was a connection between him and the older guy in the kitchen. The male in the basement liked to hang out exclusively in the male homeowner's tool room. Another investigator and I felt that this guy was an engineer in his former life, which helped explain his gravitating toward the tools. Being in that room with him made several people, and me, dizzy. None of the men felt it. I concluded he did not really have time for women, and found that making them dizzy, made them leave his area.

On the landing, at the bottom of the basement stairs, many of us felt dizzy. At first, I blamed it on the old man in the tool room just behind this area. It soon became clear the dizziness was coming from a different source. While standing there, the feeling of being watched from under the basement stairs became even stronger. I turned that way, and heard one of my team members say yes, in the direction I was looking. She was feeling a pull to that area as well. That back area was pitch-black, but I knew there were at least four, maybe five, kids standing there watching us.

By impulse, we walked in the direction of that room under the stairs. I felt the energy scatter ahead of me. I popped my flashlight on, and caught the pant leg and shoe of what looked to be a young male spirit. I also saw the hem of a dress on a female spirit. They were gone in a flash—spirits are amazing. Their story came into my mind, such a sad tale they were telling me. These children had died in a house fire on this land many years ago. They stayed here, waiting for their parents to come back for them; the youngest desperately yearned for their mom. The older children would go out, in search of their parents; these children did not know they were dead. This was incredibly emotional, for all of us. I knew in my mind, their mother had been waiting for them. We had to help them rejoin their parents.

My teammate, who is also a medium, helped me bring down the light for them to go into. She sat on the floor in the room, talking to the littlest ones, coaxing them along. A couple of them needed no words, they jumped into the light and were gone. A boy child, the third, was not far behind and was gone. I could clearly see two more children off in the shadows. The girl looked to be about fourteen years of age; she held the hand of a much younger child. Ponies being in heaven was brought up, and that is all it took—she followed the others into the light. My gut yelled to me that something was still not right. I was not sure what had happened, it looked like only the older girl stepped into the light. What happened to the younger one? There were no children left standing in the shadows. I asked everybody, in general, if they though that both had gone into the light. With apprehension, I let it go, we moved on.

Going back into the tool room, we gave the man in there a set of choices: leave, or go home, but he had to go. He refused to do either (the guy really was a pompous ass) and honestly, I was quite done with him. I told him again, you have to go, there is no choice of staying. The homeowners want you out, you will go. Since we were already doing sage work in another part of the basement, we brought it in there. I told him what would happen with the sage, he snapped an answer at me. I brought down the light for him, he turned his back. We hit him with the sage, my spirit guide ushered him up the basement stairs, out the garage door, and out into the street. Salt was laid down in that room, and at the garage doo— he was not coming back in.

Going back into the main basement, the feeling was much lighter. Even the female homeowner could tell the difference and commented on how much better it felt. She walked around the pool table, to the back corner of the basement, saying that area felt much better, too. It got my attention when she said, "Actually, last week one day, the weird, creepy feeling back here was gone." I smiled as I remembered that last week I had remotely closed a portal in that area of the basement. Between the adult male spirit and the kids, all that energy created a portal. She also said, "Well, the bedroom above this area feels better, too, hmmm!" Makes sense that it would feel better. Whatever was coming through here would use this area to go upstairs through the floor. I did not realize I had helped in so many ways.

Discussion turned to the old man in the kitchen. We needed to figure out why he was being nasty to the family on certain occasions; he would make the house smell like a rotting body every holiday.

Just as I stepped on the bottom stair to go up, something on my left caught my attention. It was a child, I knew something had not been right when his sister went into the light. Stopping so quickly, I was run into from behind. I apologized and told them why I had stopped. "He has gone back under the stairs, we need to help him." I thought he must be terrified with his parents missing, and now—his siblings as well.

Everyone turned around, all of us were talking at the same time, each concerned about the little boy. I work with some amazing people, I must say. A few of us gathered in the back room with him, and brought down the light. We were seated on the floor to become more his size, more approachable. One at a time, each of us talked to him and told him it was safe to go. I told him his mother was in the light waiting for him.

Shy, he stepped forward out of the shadows, so sweet and small. One little foot in the light, he paused and looked around at us. We all smiled, were shaking our heads, yes, go. He looked up into the light and his expression changed to a huge, happy grin. Without hesitation, he stepped in with his other foot, raised up his arms, in a pick-me-up motion. We knew he had seen his mother, this was an unspoken message to her. Up he went, out of sight.

Such a powerful thing, emotions overflowed. A lot of watery eyes, and throat-clearing in the group. This time, we tuned in to make sure all of the children and the old man from the tool room were gone. All was good, we headed upstairs.

In the kitchen, we tuned in to the house on this level. He was not in the kitchen, how odd. Tuning in to the outer edges of the house, we felt him in the master bedroom closet. The female homeowner did have some stories of events in that area of the house, specifically the master bedroom and the bathroom. Stories, too, about the dog barking at nothing all night, the toilet paper roll unwinding before her eyes, and her daughter's toys turning on—when there were no batteries in them. Those were pretty compelling events.

We saged the front of the house, and worked our way down the hall toward the bathroom and bedrooms. One of the mediums was in the master bedroom trying to reason with the old man spirit, but I knew he would not listen. The others went in the master bedroom and saged—he was already gone.

We finished the sage, and salted, so he could not go back down stairs. His world was shrinking and we felt confident about getting him out of the house, although, you never know.

Back in the kitchen, we had a talk with him. He had slipped past before the salt was laid down. He was done in the house, we all knew it. He flew past us and went outside, he was done. He had, at one time, owned a house on this property, that is why he was here. Actually, he had owned all the property in the neighborhood at one time. He had not been a nice man; no one liked him. He died alone and was furious that his body laid rotting, and no one cared enough to look for him. It was his own fault, he had driven everyone away, but he was convinced otherwise. I did not want to argue with a dead man, and told him so. He was banished to a woodpile, far out in the yard.

As it turns out, the area of the kitchen is about where his body was eventually found on the property. Makes sense, then, that he would bring the rancid smell in the house at the location. His reasoning for making the smell on the holidays, is so that someone would think of him. He spent all the holidays alone and miserable.

The homeowners finally acknowledged him. It will be interesting to me, at the next big holiday, to see if the house smells or not!

A week later, I got messages from the other investigators that were at the house with me. They had been going through their evidence and recorded voices of the dead. There was a little girl's voice recorded on the basement stairs. The word "No" and the name "Brittany" were picked up. There were also indistinguishable words picked up in the kitchen and the basement.

This was a very interesting, active haunt. These people had been living with this level of activity for years. They did not know what to do about it, until one of them read my first book and contacted me. They told me they did not want people to think them crazy—they wondered if they were crazy. It was easier, for a long time, to ignore what was going on, but it got worse. I am so glad they called.

UPDATE: The homeowners chose not to take all our advice. We did warn them that he would come back if everything was not followed. The old man did get back into the house. The smell had come back on the last two big holidays. He was also starting to attack their dog. Since then, they have sold this house and moved away. I wish them the very best in their new home

###

Chapter 7

Dreams

Dreams have always held great fascination for me. Possibly because my dreams have always been vivid, with full color and action. They have been known to sort-out problems for me, show me the future, as well as realities of situations, and sadly, to bring me warnings of imminent death.

The definition in the Google dictionary is so dull in comparison to my dreams: "A series of thought, images, sensations or emotions occurring in a person's mind during sleep." Sigmund Freud believed that dreams are the fulfillment of a repressed aspiration. He thought, that by studying dreams, it was the easiest road to understanding the unconscious activities of the mind. He considered dreams to be the guardians of sleep.

My definition, in the glossary of my second book, When The Dead Come Calling: "Sensations, emotions and pictures that happen in your mind, most actively during REM sleep". This, to me, is the definition of a basic dream. I have had many types of dreams. The following are examples of specific types, of which I personally have firsthand knowledge.

Prophetic or precognitive dream is seeing an event before it happens. To see an event in a dream, then have it happen exactly the same when you are awake.

In my book, Welcome To My Para"Normal" Life, I talk about my first-ever precognitive dream. I dreamt that my husband and I were in a strange city, boarding a small boat. The boat sinks while were are out in the middle of a large harbor.

Later that month, my husband and I flew-off on an adventure to the city of Boston, Massachusetts. We did some touring around and followed the historical trail markers. Toward the end, we went to see a national treasure, the USS Constitution. Way out on a Navy pier, tired and ready to eat, we wanted a quick way back to the city center. As it turned out, the quickest way back was to take a boat. When I spotted the boat, my breath was taken away. It was the exact boat I had dreamt about. At first, I was not sure I could ride on it. Knowing that dreams can be interpreted in different ways, I got on it. We had a great ride with a glorious view, and bonus—we did not sink! I had faith that the dream, and the boat sinking, had other meanings.

Another type of precognitive or prophetic dream that I have had several times, does not end well for others; these have foretold of death. At the time of the dreams, I did not realize these specific people would soon be dead. My dreams seem to be normal, like any other dream I have. However, that changes when I look out my childhood bedroom door, into the hallway; if there was a person floating past, they departed soon after. This has happened twice, first with my uncle and then my aunt.

When they float past the door, they appear to be in a trance; simply staring straight ahead, arms down at their sides, pale complexion, no expression in their eyes. The first dream, as I said, had been of my uncle. I had no idea at the time, what sad news I would be receiving later the next day. With the dream about my aunt, I got out of bed the next morning, thinking I knew what news was coming at some point that day. I waited by the phone, and eventually the news arrived that she had passed away.

I had this same sort of dream about one of our neighbor's father. Same type of trance look to him, but he was outdoors, not in the hallway. My husband and I were out of town and learned later that day, on social media, that he had passed away.

Another much discussed, but harder to grasp, type of dream is lucid dreaming, or astral projection. This is also referred to as an out-of-body experience, where the soul leaves the physical body, and travels to the astral planes or vibrational planes. These planes are said to be between heaven and earth. In this particular dream, I was floating in a hospital hallway, and came upon a small chair, an office chair; I thought it might be good to sit. As I did, the chair started to move. Slow at first, then faster and faster down the hall. I was facing backward, feeling a bit panicked. I came to a set of divided, swinging, stainless steel hospital doors. As I got to them, they swung open, and as I passed through them, the chair turned, so that I was facing forward. I thought, how nice to see where I am going. As that thought passed through my mind, I woke up. I said out loud, "Well, hell. I am going to lose my job!" I had looked forward, and saw what was coming. Within the month, I got laid off. It was the move that gave me the time to write my first book! This dream was actually a mix of two sorts: precognitive dreaming and astral projection. I had foretold the future, while having an out-of-body experience. I will never forget this dream, it showed me that I need to own my life and keep it moving forward.

Lucid dreaming is basically the same as an out-of-body experience. However, for me this type of dreaming is a much more vivd experience. This, too, has the feeling of floating, not walking. You have direct contact with spirits, on another plane, and you are fully aware you are dreaming.

I dreamt that I was floating across a great space of beautiful green lawn, to a big wide-open house. There were many spirits, milling about talking. It struck me, they were waiting court, waiting to be heard by the head or leader. I floated into a large hall, with a massive, ornately carved table. There, at the head of the table, sat my grandmother—they were all waiting to see her. When she was alive, I always suspected there was more to her than met the eye. It was a powerful, confirming dream. I was shown we are not so far from each other in life or death.

I wanted to share this dream because it involves my great uncle, he came to me attached to a picture. The dream does not fit into lucid nor prophetic dreaming, nor is it astral projection —I did not leave my body, they came to me. This was a visitation dream by several past family members.

I have been trying for many years to get my great uncle to leave the picture to which he is attached, and go home. I have asked him to imagine what home or heaven is to him. He let me know he was frightened at the thought of going, he thinks his God is mad at him. We have argued this point, ad nauseam. Feeling fed up with him, I let my spirit guide take the wheel and deal with us both!

In my dream, his sister (my grandmother) my aunt, and his nephew (my dad) all gather in the garage where I have him stashed. They gather around him; he is nervous, they hug him tight. A beam of white light comes down upon them all and in one move, they jettison up into the light and are gone.

Upon waking the next morning, I lay in bed, slowly opening my senses to the house. It was quiet, no extra or excess energy being produced. The house was calm and quiet for the first time in a long time.

That night I had a follow-up dream from the one the night before. The dreams were similar, but with much more detail, and a few new things added in. This time, I got out of bed and stood in the doorway to the garage. My great uncle was in the middle of the garage—full apparition—looking lost and confused. My heart was sad for him, but he would not let me help him.

He turned, looked at me and shook his head, yes. At the same time a white light descended upon him. He started to lift up off the ground, but he panicked; I could see it in his face. He changed his mind and was about to step out of the light, when my grandmother leaned-in and grabbed him by the arm from above.

I heard her say to him, "Welcome, it's about damn time!" I heard my dad's voice, saying something to his uncle, but it was indistinguishable. I could see them hug and there was the sweetest sound of them all laughing together. Love, so much love, and healing.

At that point I floated back to wakefulness. This was extremely powerful. I waited for several days and there were no sightings of my great uncle

This was too strong not to be real. When things are this strong/clear, there is no other answer for me, it happened

UPDATE: My great uncle is back! I am not able to get a definitive answer out of him why. It might be that he came back to protect me. There is a male spirit in my house, on occasion; he appears in shadow form, wearing a hat, and feels heavy.

###

Exie Susanne Smith

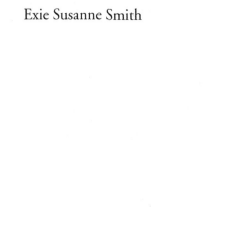

Chapter 8

Random Happenings

I was at a fabulous convention in the upper peninsula of Michigan, when something random happened! This paranormal convention lasts two days and is filled with all things paranormal and otherworldly. I have been to this event several times without anything spiritual happening. For whatever reason, this time, weird things had been happening.

It was day two, in the early afternoon. My husband had gone off to get lunch for us both. I was talking to a customer at my table, and noticed, out of the corner of my right eye, someone rapidly walking down the aisle of vendor and speaker tables. It was obvious, or maybe just my gut, that they were heading toward me. Just as this person reached my table, he suddenly made a left turn; this took him between my table and the one next to me. He turned again, and stoped right behind me. I turned to say hi, I assumed, to my husband. There was no one there. I knew it had to be him (it felt like him) but there was no one there. The spirit, whoever it was, simply faded away. That was weird!   ###

While attending the same convention in the Upper Peninsula of Michigan, I had an opportunity to present. Sadly though, for that to happen, a good friend of mine had to leave—his wife had been injured. Later in the evening, while backstage trying to get my computer presentation ready for the morning, I got a message from my spirit guide. She told me to speak up about the schedule opening in the next day's gallery readings.

My spirit guide continued to bug me until the next morning. I told her to stop, because saying something the night before did not sit comfortably with me. I told her I would I wait until the next day.

The next morning, just as I was introduced to the crowd by one of the event coordinators, I offered to do the galleries. I assumed he would think about it, and we might talk more after I was offstage, not a problem.

Walking from the theater to the room, where we all had tables set up, I was congratulated at least five times on my new gallery readings. It seems they took me up on my offer! My spirit guide was in my head telling me, "See, you just needed to step forward. Speak up and let them know you are interested. Congratulations on taking the next step in your career."

I spoke up and made this happen. In my gut, I knew I could do this, I had done a gallery reading a year or so before, and it was great. I asked a friend of mine to join me for the event. The thing that worried me was dead time during the event; I wanted the paying customers to get their money's worth.

She and I walked into the upstairs banquet room, where there were fifty to sixty people sitting in chairs waiting for us to join them. We simultaneously looked at each other, clasped hands, smiled, and walked down, towards the front, down the main aisle of chairs. The energy in the room was high, and sweet, it felt right. In my mind, I was thinking this is such a crap shoot, but stayed confident that it was going to work out.

We introduced ourselves. Next, we gave the audience a basic rundown on how (we thought) the next hour was going to go, and then started to open ourselves up. I could feel spirits lining-up to come in; so many of them wanted to communicate with the people in this room!

A first-ever, for me, was that I was getting names from my spirit guide. I told the gallery the name/names I was getting… Tim or Timothy. The other medium turned and looked at me —like I was insane. She quietly said, "What is this? You don't get names?"

I smiled, "Well, apparently, I do now!" We started to laugh, she shook her head, and I kept the reading going.

The stronger spirits were coming in first, as always. I repeated the name of the men I was getting and several people raised their hands. I did not like that so many hands went up, and it was certainly not expected. Now, I had to give clues as to whom was coming forward. Tuning in more, I pulled details from the spirit and gave those, a couple hands went down. That was good, but, there were still two people, on opposite sides of the room, with their hands up. A few more details were shown to me, then there was only one hand left up—spirit had an unexpected message of love. For the sake of privacy, I am not going to disclose certain parts of the readings. Even though spirit delivered the messages with others around, they are their stories to share, not mine.

Shockingly, the hour was over before we knew it. Many new experiences happened in that short amount of time. The other medium and I were both pleased, and honored, at how many spirits we were able to bring through.

We were both over-the-moon at how the gallery turned out! The energy and love in the room was overwhelming, once we slowed down enough to notice it. She and I hugged, and looked at each other, with love and respect; it was a life-affirming moment. Nothing for me, spiritually, would ever be the same again.

There were many hours left in the day, and I hoped I would not be completely drained of energy before it was over. Out of the blue, an idea came to mind. Why don't I consult with my spirit guide about her helping me with my energy. Use her as a battery so I do not drain myself. I did just that, and it worked incredibly well.

The next day of the convention, off we went—upstairs to do our gallery reading. From the area outside the banquet room, we could see through the double doors. What we saw stopped us dead in our tracks. The room was even more crowded than yesterday! Again, we locked hands, and walked into the room as the double doors clicked shut behind us. It was touching to hear the audience gasp as we entered the room, which brought on misty eyes for both of us. We were honored and touched by their excitement.

From the front of the room, with huge smiles on our faces, we introduced ourselves. We let the gallery know how we thought ,and prayed, how the next hour would go. I had hoped that spirits would not show up again today, in multiples, as they had yesterday. No, that would have been too easy. Again, many people raised their hands for each name I miraculously pulled out of my mind. More deciphering of clues, but honestly it turned out to be great fun, and a huge learning experience for me. During the readings, I glanced at the clock (at a time I thought was about halfway through)…there were only minutes left in the hour! How did the time go by so quickly?

At one point, I had spirits coming through that no one was claiming; I thought to myself, what the hell do I do now? No one was picking up on the clues these spirits were giving. I knew better than to think their attendance was a mistake. These spirits were not leaving until they were heard.

I said to the gallery, "The two spirits that have come through, I know they belong to someone in this room. The details are too specific, and too many, for that not to be true." It crossed my mind that someone was simply too afraid to speak up. I understood that it might be frightening to go out-on-a-limb in front of a group of people.

At that point, I had to move on; I was worried that people would get bored if I stayed on one line too long. I held out hope that someone would realize, or be brave, and speak up. For other spirits to come in, for me, I had to move these two out of the way. I looked up and saw that the ceiling had a drop down—it looked like bench seating to me. I think the name for it is coffered ceiling. Out loud, I asked these two spirits to have a seat on that bench-looking detail on the ceiling, and we would get back to them! I said it aloud so the gallery would understand just what I was doing. The spirits understood, and kindly flew to a spot in the corner of the ceiling.

The gallery got a huge kick out of this, especially when I said, "Stay, please!" I dubbed it the waiting room.

Everyone, including the other medium, laughed. In fact, she turned, looked at me, and asked laughingly, "Who are you?" I shrugged and grinned back!

The rest of the gallery reading went fantastic! We were pleased we had so many spirit family members and friends come through. I am not sure I have ever had an hour go faster. We concluded the event with many thanks to the gallery, the spirits, their spirit guides, and ours.

Several people stayed behind with us, they had great questions. Finally someone claimed the spirits on our ceiling waiting room. I was so relieved when this shy person spoke up to tell us that those spirits were connected to her brother.

She said the elaborate details I wove, while in my trance-like state, of the male and female were too spot-on for her to ignore. The thing that threw her, was that she thought spirit only came through for family and friends that had a direct connection. It took her a few moments to realize that even though they had nothing to do with her directly, it was still a story that touched her life.

The messages were great! He came through to apologize. And, the female spirit came to vent at him for his past sins—it was her ex-husband!

It was a good reminder for us, in our next galleries, that we needed to inform gallery members that spirit will find a way to get a message across; no one wants to be forgotten.

A friend of mine recored that session and sent it all to me. I had never thought to do this, what a great idea! The following is just some of what was picked up. There were many voices talking at one point, but none of them distinguishable. I was so sad; there were entire groups of the dead talking about our comments and connections. My name was spoken. Then the name "Henry," followed by, "better." At one point during the gallery, we were talking about lost children, and on the recording, you could hear children talking. There were no children in the banquet room during the gallery. There was a whistle in reply to a comment I made about a certain spirit. I laughed aloud at that; someone was impressed! There were several deep, male voices on the recording. One of them said, "Can't" to a question, and the other said, "No."

These were not earth shaking conversations on the recorder. However, I cannot discount them—they were realtime conversations, and answers to questions we posed. That was cool! I will use a recorder at all my gallery readings.

Have you ever gone by a house, glanced at it, and a light goes on in a room? Or, a light on the front porch goes on whenever you go by? Usually, it feels fairly random and I let it go. I do not believe in coincidence. I guess I could possibly chalk it up to being in the right place at the right time. What do you say about this if it's happened to you, during your entire lifetime?

My favorite of all these occurrences is when I was a kid, about eight or nine. We used to rent a cottage on the shores of Lake Michigan in Grand Haven. Up on the top of the bluff, to the north of our cottage, was an amazing, old Victorian home. Even in its eery state of dilapidation, she was beautiful and fascinating to me.

When on the beach, I used to look at the house and imagined who lived there. I pictured the parties that were held, and what they were wearing. I could hear conversation and music. I know, now, it was not my imagination. I know I was really seeing the spirits that inhabited the house.

One evening, a group of us were out on the beach, having a bonfire. I glanced up at that old house, like I always did, but this time, there was something different. In the living room, it appeared as if there was a light on. It illuminated the room and shone through the window frame. As I said something about it to the others aloud, they turned—and the light went out. They questioned, "Which window? You're kidding right?" Then, they simply resorted to making fun of me. I tried once to profess my innocence, but found it of no use. I simply laughed with them, like I had played a joke.

At breakfast, not being able to let it go, I told my parents about what I had seen. They both chimed-in that it must have been an intruder with a flashlight. My dad somehow knew that there was no electricity in the old house. He also commented that there was no glass in the windows of the house—no one has lived there for years.

Thinking about it for most that day, I decided they must be correct, that someone was simply trespassing, being nosy. I decided to just let it go. I stopped bringing it up; people had started to look at me weirdly. I know what I saw, that would have to suffice. I was learning not to believe, not to acknowledge who I really was, to forget.

For the next week, I sat on the beach, facing the old house, up on the bluff, my imagination playing out past events that took place in the house. Grand parties, fights between the husband and wife, cocktail hour, and the cook in the kitchen complaining about everything. It was a lonely house—sad— even when it had been full of people and music.

I knew the light coming on, in the house, had been for me. An acknowledgement of the little girl down on the beach, with abilities that she did not understand, and would not for many years to come. They knew me before I did. They knew it was me coming into their place to eavesdrop on them; they also knew I did not realize I was doing it.

We returned to that same cottage for many summers after that. As hard as I wished, I was never again able to see the light turn on in the living room of the old house again... it will stay in my mind forever, though. It was special, just like that little girl.

###

Chapter 9

All Will Be Revealed

It had been a day filled with the weirdest happenings. I had a feeling there was a purpose, and eventually that purpose would reveal itself. For now, all I could do was hold on and wait.

My cell phone rang, and on the other end was a woman I had not talked to for many years. Her deceased husband had worked, and been good friends with my husband. Several years after her husband retired, he became ill; it was tragic. We talked on the phone for a few minutes, then she mentioned she was in the area for an appointment, and she asked to come by the house.

It was nice to see her; she really had not changed. It soon became evident that she had mostly came to see me, not my husband. He left to run errands so she could say what she needed. Conversation flowed along, and eventually turned to what I had been doing in the years since we had last seen each other, "I have written and published two books about the paranormal. Last fall, I started doing readings as a medium."

I carefully watched her facial expressions and body language for a response to what I had just said. I expected her to say, "Oh, well that's nice, I have to go!" Shame on me for judging what her reaction might be. To my surprise, she proceeded to tell me two paranormal events that happened to her granddaughter.

It turned out, she was living north of me, in a sweet town that my husband and I happen to frequent for dinner. Her granddaughter is a server in a local establishment, and lives just down the street in an old house that had been converted to apartments. The more she talked about the old house, the more uncomfortable I became for her granddaughter. I knew the basement of the place was bad—it was glaring at me. The feeling was so strong. Before she left, I asked her to have her granddaughter call me, at some point, that day. I was being told by my spirits that it was important, and there was no time to waste.

After her granddaughter's shift was over, she did, indeed, call me. Right off, she said, "I am surprised by your message. I just had my apartment saged by a medium." Knowing spirit can linger for a day or two after a cleansing, I inquired how long it had been since that was done. "It has been at least a week." That was far too long ago for this to be leftover energy of a removed spirit; this was something else. So, I really tuned in to the house, using her phone to get even closer. I picked up three spirits in the house in total. I knew at least one spirit was in her apartment; the others were close by—and also in her apartment on occasion. There was an older woman, the original homeowner, she resides in an upstairs apartment. Then there was a cranky old man, who mostly stayed in the cellar, but did enter her apartment, just to nose around.

Not wanting to cut-up the other medium, I made sure the young woman knew that the medium had done a good job of cleansing her apartment. There were simply a few things that should have been done along with it, that she did not do. Attention was only paid to that apartment, not the building as a whole, which it used to be. Apparently, she did not lay down salt as she saged. And, as she moved from room to room—so did the spirits—staying away from her and the smoke. Spirits are clever that way!

The old woman spirit stays upstairs with an elderly woman. The spirit woman used to own the house. She loves the place and will never leave, and her favorite place is the top floor. I inquired if there was an older woman who lived upstairs. The young lady was shocked that I knew that, and wanted to know how I knew. "How can you tell all this over the phone? We live pretty far apart."

"It is one of my abilities. I use energy from things so my messages are stronger." I continued to tell her the old lady spirit rarely comes downstairs; she likes the view of town from the second floor! I mentioned a little boy being in her apartment. "He likes you because you are young. He likes to hang out in the kitchen. Have you ever gotten out of bed to find the knobs on the gas stove turned on?"

"Oh, my God! You are blowing me away. Yes, I have had that happen. That is one of the reasons I had the medium come in. It is a gas stove; I was afraid I would asphyxiate or the place would blow-up. The medium said was gone."

"No, he is not gone. He also likes to sit on the stairs that go from your kitchen, to the cellar below the house."

"There are no stairs that go from my kitchen to the cellar."

I know they are there, I can see them. What she does not realize, is that they are behind the wall her microwave is on. I did not say this, though, I did not want to totally freak her out!

The last spirit I was picking up was that of a nasty crabby old man who likes to hang-out in the cellar. It is a perfect place for his bad personality—dark, damp and dirty. I thought, maybe this was the reason the basement was causing me distress. It was a feeling I could not shake, and that bothered me. I knew there was something down there waiting to cause a problem, but what, or whom?

Trying to get my point across, just how strongly I felt there was something bad in, or about, the cellar. I thought if I gave her an example of how it felt to me, she would catch-on. I said, "The cellar feels, to me, like it is going to blow. It's like you have a large pot of potatoes on the stove to boil, and the lid closed too tightly. It will boil over and make a mess."

She said, "There is no key to the cellar, so I cannot go down to check it out."

We completed the phone conversation, after setting a date and time for me to come see the old house and her apartment. The next day she called me, "I got a key to the cellar."

"Great! So, when I come over, we can cleanse down there as well."

The following day, she called me again. "I went down into the cellar—it smelled real strong of gas. I called the gas company, and they came out immediately. They found five gas leaks, and were able to fix them all."

Now, I understood why my spirit guide was being so urgent about that area. Also, why I saw the imagery of the lid blowing-off and the pot overflowing. That house could have blown-up at any time. I trusted what I was being shown, and informed her. It is a repeating message, a life message.

I was supposed to go to her apartment the next morning, but was thinking it possibly could be a waste of time, and almost canceled. The gas leaks had been fixed, and I did, remotely, close a portal in the wall where the basement stairway comes up. The one she never knew existed, too funny! The three spirits in the house were harmless. I texted her the info, and what I was thinking. Her reply was, "Please still come and check the entire house with your abilities."

One of the funny aspects of this, was the next morning, when I got into my car to drive to her apartment—the radio immediately changed songs. The song that came on was Highway to Hell! I rolled my eyes, laughed, and pulled away singing. On the way to her apartment, I tuned my abilities in on the place, making sure nothing had changed... in a bad way. Nothing had changed, and the spirits had no idea I was headed in their direction. That is always a plus.

When I pulled into the back parking lot, I knew there was a spirit in the window watching me. They must have picked up on her nerves, and the intentions being put out. I could sense the old woman spirit on the top floor, looking at me out a window. She was fine; just curious as to who pulled into her little world. The spirit of the little boy was at the kitchen window of my client's apartment. He wondered about me, but was not worried. As I went up the back porch steps to knock on the door, he rushed to the cellar. The grumpy old man was in the cellar as well. He was stewing over my arrival and wondering what he could do about me. He soon realized there was nothing he could do, and I felt him rush to the back of the cellar to hide. He was sending out a message to me, "Take pity on me, I am just an old man." All I could think was, his time is limited. Once he was gone, the entire place would feel much lighter.

She greeted me and opened the door so I could enter. I told her what was up with her apartment, spiritually, and got to work. I saged the three rooms of her apartment—it felt great and looked brighter. She thought so, too, and was shocked. In the kitchen, I had a talk with the little boy, who thought he had snuck back in. I told him no more playing with knobs on the stove. I asked if his intention was to kill the young woman in this apartment. His energy gave off a no. I told him, "Then knock it off, or you just might kill her with your game." She asked me not to send him away, not a problem, she is paying the rent. What I did not tell her, was I told the boy, through telepathy, that if he did not listen to me, I would come back and send him home! I needed him to understand the severity of this situation—he did. My job at this point, was to keep her alive. While we were in the kitchen, I turned to the blank wall, the one the microwave was on, and told her the cellar stairway door used to be there. She had no idea they were there, and honestly had no reason to know.

We had to go out of her apartment, and into the yard, to get into the cellar; not uncommon with old houses. Into the dark, damp cellar we stepped. The old grumpy man was still hiding, so-to-speak. I pointed out the stair ahead of us, and that they dead-ended into her kitchen wall. She was shocked, she had not believed me. She never thought I could know that there were stairs that used to go to her kitchen… not over the phone!

Getting the items out of my travel bag, I fired up the sage, said a prayer, and went off, to my right, to get things started. It was a small area (no air moved) so I did not use salt to divide the areas. There was no place for this old man's spirit to go; he was trapped and not happy about it. Moving my way over to the left, where the old man was hiding, in an old storage closet, I opened the door. Even shining my flashlight into the space was of no use, the light did not penetrate him at all. I told her that it was the spirit of the old man; he is trying to fill the space with darkness to look intimidating. She said, "I cannot see into to that little room at all. I should be able to, it's tiny." I was glad she noticed that, it helped convince her that spirit was still around the house. I made sure she understood that he was much more afraid of us, and that he was all bluster.

I walked into the entrance of the storage room as I fanned sage into the area. Just before the sage would have reached him, he went out the back wall of the storage unit. You can run but you cannot hide. I stepped around the little room and kept saging toward him. He was very weak by the time we got him in the last corner of the basement. He said some nasty words to me—his true character came out—just as the sage took him away. I chuckled softly as I said a silent bye-bye!

She had tried to convince me that he needed to stay. I explained to her that he was a user of energy from the house, and from her. I told her she would find that she has much more energy in the days to come. The cellar was clean and would stay that way. We headed back up, out into the fresh air.

While we were standing in the backyard area, through telepathy, I told the old woman spirit on the top floor that she was welcome to stay. There was one stipulation; she could no longer travel around the house, and to just stay in the top floor apartment. I also asked if she would please be the spirit-monitor for the entire house, and if any new spirits showed-up, to let me know. She would know without being in the areas. She was happy to be of service, she felt useful and liked that fact.

I was satisfied with this cleansing and the investigation that ran simultaneously. The house was good, and the spirits that were staying, were in-hand.

###

Exie Susanne Smith

Chapter 10

Love & Light

During a recent house blessing, I encountered a first! I was saging the basement of a home, dedicating it to love, light, and the higher power. While working my way around the perimeter, I approached a dark, shadowy storage room. Bending forward to make sure my feather moved sage below some hanging items, a black object rapidly moved toward me out of the darkness, from out of the back of the closet. This thing was half human and half dog, on all fours, coming at me with teeth bared. It moved quickly toward my left leg, as if to bite me. Out of instinct, as this thing leaped for my leg, I fanned sage smoke at it. The moment the smoke hit, it yipped with a wrenching noise and, the inhuman thing disappeared.

The homeowner, who was a few feet away, asked, "What just happened? I felt a rush of something, then it was gone." I told her what I just witnessed. She apologized to me. I laughed, and told her not to apologize, "This is why I am here." That seemed to be the end of him. As I went through the rest of the basement, it felt heavy, but at least there were no more demon-animals running at me out of the dark.

I do think he was a byproduct of some issues in the house that have yet to be dealt with. There is depression in the home that is not being taken care of. If not, more things like this will manifest. I was honest with the homeowner and told her what to watch for. I pray for them.

The first warm day of spring had arrived. It was clear, and full of all things new. Little did I realize, how new and different everything, including the weather, was going to be.

I was off to the salon to get my hair trimmed. Walking through the door of the salon felt as if I had passed through a veil of illness. This feeling draped over me like a wet cloth, from head to toe. I immediately had to sit down; glad for a chair close to me. As I sat there, my eyes were drawn to a door about twenty feet in front of me. From my previous visits, I knew this was the restroom for salon customers. I also knew my ill-feeling was coming from inside that room.

One of the salon's stylists walked over to the door and knocked on it. She asked, whomever was inside, if they were all right? There was no reply. The stylist turned to her left, looking at the receptionist, and asked for direction on what to do next? A good question, since there still had been no answer from inside the room. The receptionist suggested trying the door knob—the door was locked. Just then, there was a click. The person inside was unlocking the door; that made us all feel a bit better. When the stylist opened the door, the salon filled with even more heaviness. Then, it became hard to breathe.

My stylist came over to greet me and take me to her station. I could hardly stand and walk; she literally had to help me. She took a good look at me in the mirror and asked, "What the hell is wrong?"

I asked a question back, "What the hell is going on in here?"

"A customer took prescription medication and had a bad reaction to it."

I inquired, "What did she take? It must have been a fairly heavy drug, at least it feels that way."

The reply shocked me, "Her stylist told me she said it was an oxycontin! The first one didn't work, so she took a second one! It looks as if they are both working now, because she was just ill in the bathroom."

I told my stylist, "Once this woman leaves, go to the back and say some prayers to bring your shop back to a normal, healthy balance."

My next appointment, about a month later, my stylist told me she did as I instructed and the salon felt immediately better.

I know she was surprised that it worked—I was impressed that she actually tried it!

I never had anything like this happen to me. It hit me like a car at a high rate of speed. I also never had the courage to speak to someone about what I was feeling. It was obvious that the entire salon of people were feeling something off in the place.

I was proud that I spoke-up, and offered a suggestion on how to remedy the situation. I am pleased it helped, and that they did not lose any customers. The feeling was so strong…it very easily could have harmed their business.

When someone calls for help to rid a spirit from their home, you go as soon as possible. When it is members of your close inner-circle of friends, and their animals are being threatened, you drop everything and go.

Great friends of ours had been having an occasional issue at their home, honestly, for a bit too long. I suggested, about a year ago, they get rid of the spirit in the basement. Every time the basement spirit subject came up, they countered with statements of, "He is shy, he really does not bother us. He stays in the basement, and the animals are just fine with him." I would shake my head and chuckle with them.

These two are the hardest-working, busiest couple we know. I do understand that a house cleansing takes time, which they are hard-pressed to find. I have been in their shoes as well—the spirit is not bothering us—we can let him be. I also, now, understand what can happen when you leave a spirit in your home. For the time being, I let the topic drop. I knew eventually they would get back to me for help, or at least have a good story about it!

A private message on social media popped-up, the tagline read: "weirdness big-time in the basement." I smiled and checked my calendar for the weekend next, which was only a few days away. Opening the message, she had a list of new weirdness happening in the house and basement: bad odor, heavy feeling, overwhelming sadness, being watched, being followed, being pushed, the cat being bothered, and the dogs flipping-out, barking nonstop at the basement stairs.

We settled on a date for me to come over and help them clean this mess up. I asked her to make some saltwater. Recently, a friend of mine had me make some to use while doing a cleansing in my own home. I used it on the walls, and then simply sprayed it in the air in the room after I had saged. It was a great finishing touch. The room's light was even brighter afterward.

Once our typed conversation was finished, I tuned in to their house with my abilities. This has to be done with care, for a few reasons. I would never intrude on the privacy of someone's home unless necessary, let me get that straight. The other reasons, are that I need to know what I am soon to come face-to-face with, so-to-speak and, I want to know their power, their mind. Are they preparing for me, are they growing stronger? I am as careful as possible, not to be detected by them. I do not want them attaching to me or following me out of this peek-in. I have had that happen, and choose not to repeat what was not a fun adventure.

While tuned in, I sensed there was a new spirit in the basement, along with the original one. This new one is dark in mood, attitude, and attire. He was in the center of the basement, hovering midair. One arm was attached to the ceiling, which happened to be directly under their bed. His other arms stretched-out to the walls, north, south, and east. The arms looked like they had billowing, black fabric over them —long, creepy, yet elegant fabric arms.

It did look as if he was coming up out of the floor drain. As I took a closer look, I noticed they had two floor drains. Who has two floor drains, so close together? I had seen enough, I closed my viewing and sealed it. Then, I sent a message to my friend asking, "Why do you have two floor drains in the basement?"

Her immediate reply, "How do you know we have two drains in the basement floor?" I smiled, and was rewarded with a one word reply from her, "Duh!"

Laughing, I called her cell phone; she needed to hear the creepy parts in person. "I saw something getting stronger. The original ghost is cowering in the old coal room. Plus, added bonus, this new one is creating a thing, like a sidekick. It wants company, a companion.

A deflated, "What?" was all I got from her.

I hated saying it again. "He is creating another thing, I'm totally getting the word companion. He hopes it will do his bidding around your house."

"Oh shit, we do not need him having a helper around the house. Does this mean more work when we get together?"

"No, what we are planning will do the trick. I will keep an eye on him."

I could not have agreed more with her sentiment; we did not need another thing to get rid of. We ended the conversation with me telling her, "Hang tight, do not let this thing know we are coming for him. Keep the animals safe—you guys, too. We will be there to take care of this situation in a couple days." When I said we, I was referring to our other team investigator and medium; she would be meeting us at the house.

The day had arrived for our investigation and cleansing. I gathered my bag of goodies, including the entire container of salt. In my bag, I have a shell, feather, oil, and enough sage to cleanse the neighborhood. Each of these extra items are for added safety, especially salt. You might leave a job incomplete, and then spirits can come back. I salt as I sage, that way the room you just saged, is sealed from spirit going back in. As I was packing up, I was thinking about my friends and their house. I tuned in on the basement—this thing had changed. He was still in the same form and location, but he seemed lower in the room. He was not floating as high in the area, and he was weaker. He seemed depressed, too. I tuned out.

This left me with questions: What was going on with him? Was he toying with me? Had he realized I had been checking on him, so he posed weaker? I tuned in to him several more times during the day, trying to catch him the way he was initially. He was the same every time: weak, low in the room, depressed. This was very odd to me, so I kept a wary eye on him.

Not trusting something that I know had ill-intent, a couple days earlier, for my friends I kept my plans the same. I thought perhaps he was playing a game; he wanted me to come in weaker, so he had a fighting chance. Not going to happen.

The group met in the backyard to finalize our plan. Where to start saging, what we were saying as a prayer, and how to respond if the spirit provoked.
During this, we asked the homeowners, "How much work have you done to this house since you bought it?"

"We have redone everything. Every single thing you see, inside and out, has been touched by us."

As stories of the house's history were told, I knew exactly who we were dealing with in the basement. The last story was about a family, two parents and their son, who had lived there. And, when the parents died, the son stayed. He was a drug addict, and he had stripped the house of all the copper and metals for drug money. He ended-up living in one tiny area of the basement—and he died there. BINGO!

My mouth dropped open; they knew exactly what it meant. We had our answer—this was our depressed, lonely ghost—the son. He was weak, tired of fighting to stay, and he was ready to go. He had looked for love in his life, and tried to fit in, but never found love, or friendship, not even in death.

My plans to seek-and-destroy this thing, without hesitation, had changed a bit. My approach was going to have some compassion tossed-in; I might be the first-ever to show him any. I would first ask him, with telepathy, to leave. If he said yes, then, would he like help getting home? I confused him, but thought once we started to sage, he would understand, and possibly take me up on my offer.

As we started saging in the very back of the finished basement, I spotted a picture on a shelf. "Oh my God, check-out this picture!" It was a small, 5x5, hand-drawn coincidentally by another friend. It depicted the exact form the ghost had assumed (the face was a bit different) but almost exact. It was similar to a squid with tentacles stretched out, wearing the same all-black, billowy clothing. This blew me away! Hell, it blew us all away.I looked up and thanked my spirit guide for directing me to this picture across the room, high upon a shelf. I felt pity for this ghost; he was lost, sad, and lonely.

The prayers were said, protection brought-in, sage lit, salt sprayed, and salt laid. The ghost grew weaker with each passing second, and was cornered with each succeeding bit of salt spread. In my mind, I told him to go home, find peace at last. He turned in his last bit of space, looked at me, his eyes saying thank you, and he was gone. Blinking rapidly, so the tears stayed in my eyes, we kept going. We saged and salted the rest of the house to ensure his passages back in were all closed.

My heart was heavy with relief, and a bit sad for this man. I had been privy to his lonely painful existence. All the hurt and despair he endured, it was immense. My final prayer of the evening was for him, asking God to hold him, let him know he is loved and safe, then to please lead him to the waiting arms of his parents.

Looking around the circle of my friends, I was so proud of them for the amazing work that had been done. In my heart, I know that each one of them is a great person, and certainly a blessing to me.

###

My plan had been for the last event to be the final in the book. That changed when the above event morphed into something more, something quite unbelievable.

We sat outside after we finished the house blessing, just chatting. I was facing the back of the house, and on the other side of the wall was the basement stairs. Then, the house tuned into me—letting me know that something was left unfinished inside. I saw a solid, black mass hovering above the third step; the top one was salted, it cannot pass. I was confused by what I was seeing. I cleansed that house, had felt it was clean, yet there was another mass?

My immediate reaction was to bind him, and hope it was residual energy that would go away in a few hours. This spirt was very entrenched in the house, so residual energy left over was possible. In my gut I knew better, but I had to let it play out.

The next morning, my phone rang. It was the friend whose house we had been at the night before. "Hey, I've got creepy news. This morning, as I stood watching, two of my pie plates were pushed-off my dining room table; they hit the floor and broke. My male dog, as of this morning, has completely stopped eating. What the hell?"

"Stopped eating?"

"He has not eaten a full serving of his food for several weeks, and now, he is not eating at all. Plus, neither of the dogs will leave the top of the basement stairs. They just stare down into the basement, making defensive noises. As you know Emma can't hear, so it's not that they are reacting to sound."

At this point, I had to tell her what I saw last night. I was correct, and should have listened to my gut. He was still there; very powerful, evil, and now, angry.

I was feeling angry myself. This thing is terrorizing my friends and apparently trying to kill one of the dogs. This thing needs to be destroyed, and promptly. We ended our conversation.

Immediately after, I received a text from a friend down south, "Got a minute?" She called me and questioned me about the thing in my friend's basement. This took me aback, until I remembered talking to her about it a few days earlier. I was thinking, damn, girl, you are really tuning in well these days! She said something that totally confused me, "You don't remember, do you?" I had no idea to what she was referring. She said it again, when I remained silent, "You don't remember? You don't remember the evil spirit I captured in the home of my dying friend down here?"

I did remember, but did not put the two events in the same category. She waged a major battle with an evil spirit in her friend's cellar. We both agreed that this thing was the reason her friend died. I had put her in-touch with a shaman, that I had meet back in 2012, in Lexington, Kentucky. She needed to know the steps to ride the house of such a dark, evil entity. He told her, step-by-step, how to carefully capture evil in a stone or crystal. It was fascinating, and certainly new territory for the both of us.

She shocked me when she said, "What you have been dealing with in their basement, is evil. It is called a Wendigo. This thing is a cannibal, a monster. It is an evil spirit, that is almost God-like in nature, very strong. I searched the computer for Wendigo while we chatted. The Cree Indian translation of the word Wendigo is "evil that devours." Oh my God!

Whatever is in my friend's basement, its end goal is to devour them all. He has already started with the male dog, and he is making fast work of it. This thing has wreaked havoc on this family, using their currently stressful lives against them.

Much of the information on a Wendigo is of a folklore nature, strictly written for entertainment. However, the Native American tribes of the Northeast, and Great Lakes states, talk about him in real terms; I cannot discount that. My proof of his existence was written, long ago, how to rid places and dispose of him. It would have never been written, if there were no need for it.

I am thankful my friend was open and willing to share, in detail, how to dispel the evil from my friends' home. Though our demons were of a similar nasty nature, our experiences were going to be our own. I say this because evil is not specific, it is what it wants, and needs to be, at the time. There is no predicting what a demon will do.

Preparing to do battle at this level of the spiritual world was all consuming. I was fighting for the lives of my friends. I was given a list of the items I would need. They consisted of four types of crystals, a large trapping stone/crystal, sage, cedar, sweet grass, anointed water or oil, all my guides, and God.

I entered the house and right away threw down black salt on the top step of the stairs; he could not come past there. I needed time to get my items ready to smudge, and to lay the crystals in a specific pattern around the large stone.

Filling my shell with the dried items, I then went back outside to say a prayer of protection and smudge. We then came in and did the same for all three of the animals. I also put an imaginary bubble of protection around each of the animals —just an added bit—it could not hurt.

As we descended the basement stairs, the air was noticeably stagnant, the room looked abnormally dark, and it felt heavy. My skin stood-up in goose bumps as I turned at the bottom of the stairs. The evil spirit and I made eye contact. He was summing-me-up with nasty looks. All for nothing, because I was doing the same back at him. I am glad he did not appear so the homeowner could see him, it would have possibly been too much. He was saving energy, so stayed in this current, mostly invisible form.

The evil spirit backed-up as we approached the center of the room. I wanted to lay the stones halfway between the front and back walls of the basement. We had his interest, that was good. We set the center stone, the trapping stone, down on the floor, and then added the other crystals in a set-pattern all the way around. I was sensing, from him, that he assumed this was an offering from the homeowners, in an effort to save their lives. He was emitting this was marvelous, but was going to kill them anyway. Ego, it will get you in trouble every time. I was counting on it.

Once the crystals were laid, I concentrated on the center stone. In it, mentally, I created a well. Out of the well, I pulled up a vortex. This vortex would work much like a lobster trap: once you are in, you are not getting out. The vortex would hold him, and with him struggling to get out, it would work him in deeper. As he moved down into the stone, the vortex would close-up behind him. The final event would be the vortex sealing over, trapping him inside. With those intentions set, I mentally baited the trap by putting a drop of blood in the center cavity of the trapping stone. He is a carnivore, so a snack might be appealing to him! At the last minute, I had a thought —I prayed that the cat wouldn't come down and use the crystals for floor hockey. I asked the good spirits present to help with that.

The last thing we had to do, for now, was thank the evil spirit. It took some time wrapping our heads around this part. We thanked him for the lessons that he offered-up for all of us to learn. We then told him, those lessons have been learned, your work here is done. It is time for you to go. This beautiful large crystal is our gift to you, your personal vessel. Come and see for yourself how beautiful and special it is.

I was told the crystal would let me know when the trapping was done; when the spirit was fully engulfed and trapped. This would take three and five days to complete. Upon hearing this statement, "The stone will let you know!" I stopped the conversation, I needed time to comprehend. I am now to communicate with a rock? I smiled, because in the store, when I was looking for the perfect crystal to purchase, it spoke to me then. How will I explain this one to my husband?

Going over my checklist, everything had to be done, step-by-step, nothing could be missed. Crystals were set, intentions were set on them, and a bubble was placed around the basement to keep distractions away from the spirit. I wanted him to only have eyes for the morsel of blood in the stone—and go in after it.

Moving upstairs, we took the dogs outside to cleanse them, and us, with the smudge smoke. I took the remaining smolder in the house to put some over the cat. It was sweet, the smoke went over her and she started to purr. It had been an interesting day!

I left, heading for home. Once there, I took a bath in

Epsom salts to do a final cleanse on myself; I had the homeowners do the same. As I drove home, I could not resist tuning my abilities back into the basement of the house. I hoped I would find the spirit as enthralled with his gift as he had been when I left. Happily, he was. He was staring at the large stone, circling all the way around it, in the air. I tuned out and shut the path so he could not find a way to me.

The homeowner sent me a picture of the two dogs sleeping in the living room. Cute, but I did not understand the significance of it, until I read her attached note. "First time in many weeks they have left the top of the stairs. No more standing guard." Loved this news. That meant to me the house was healing, freeing itself from the monster.

Another text arrived, from the homeowner, an hour later. "Monkey just ate a full meal, he hasn't done that in two weeks and in fact, had stopped eating completely this morning." She was referring to her male bulldog, who would probably eat twenty-four hours a day, if you let him. The evil spirit was intending on him being the first victim, I have no doubt of that. I think the spirit thought Monkey posed the biggest threat. Great news—things were continuing in the right direction.

Late that night, just before I turned-out my light to sleep, I checked on the spirit. It appeared a portion of him had gotten pulled in by the vortex. It looked as if the tip, or end, of his long flowing robe was moving its way down the vortex. The end had begun.

The next morning, I tuned back in, and could not have been happier. He was about a quarter of the way into the trap. I really wanted to relax, but knew better. I kept talking to him and the stone, thanking them both for the honor of the lessons, and his duty to humanity.

At 3:43 a.m., the morning of the third day, the crystal woke me up with a message. "It is done." Tuning my senses in to the basement, showed me he was truly gone and I could feel him inside the crystal. The intentions had worked, the vortex sealed him inside, as he entered. Clean and neat, that is the way I like it. I thanked the crystal for letting me know, and for its outstanding service.

In the morning, at a proper hour, I let the homeowner know it was done. I had happened to mention the time I was informed by the stone. She said she thought it might have been about 7:45 a.m. Their male bulldog had let out a loud howl at that time. This hit me as being all wrong. That was not a normal reaction from that dog, ever.

I knew my crystal was correct with its information, so what was this about? I wondered, with all this dog has been through, was he trying to tell us something Just to be safe, I tuned my abilities in to their home, not just the basement. "I will be damned!" In the basement, in the back half, there was another dark spirit. I remembered at that point, the evil spirt had been creating a sidekick, a helper. Looks like he had finished, and was ready to step into his master's newly vacated shoes.

No way was this going to happen to my friends, no way. Tuning in to the trapping stone, I needed to see if there was room for two spirits, there was. Mentally, I added another drop of blood into a cavity that I created. The spirit in the other room was apparently hungry because he instantly showed-up next to the stone. Seizing they opportunity, I made a path to the blood in the stone. In my mind, I grabbed the spirit and thrust him into the stone, and sealed it as he entered. Done and done!

With the trapping complete, I needed to get to the stone—it must be removed from the home as soon as possible.

A few different supplies were needed for removal. The stone needs to be placed into a bag of sand, covered over, and sealed shut. Without haste, it is to be taken from the house, and buried someplace away from the homeowners. The other crystals were collected. Some would be buried on the property, the rest will be cleansed, and can be used again.

The last steps after the trapping stone was removed, was to smudge the house one last time (pets, too), use the oils, and create a larger bubble over and under the entire house.

I want to thank my friend, the shaman in Kentucky, for teaching us, and for sharing without hesitation. I also want to thank my girlfriend from Tennessee: you shared without hesitation as well. The information, you both shared and taught, saved lives and brought a family closer. Thank you from the bottom of my heart.

###

GLOSSARY

Ascended Masters
Souls that have become enlightened or transformed. Ascended to higher levels of consciousness.

Automatic Writing or Typing
Writing or typing that occurs without the knowledge of the person doing the action.

Clairaudient or Clear Hearing
The ability to hear voices, sounds, and/or music that is not audible to the normal ear.

Clairvoyant or Clear Seeing
The ability to receive things that are not visible with the normal eye. Is someone who receives intuitive messages visually from the spirit; also known as a Medium.

Cover or Protection
To visualize walls, fabric, or doors over or around you. The items used/visualized are up to you, and what you need at the time. Whatever it takes to stop unseen feelings, spirits or spells from reaching you, harming you, clouding your mind, or draining your energy.

Crown Chakra
This is located on the top of your head, the crown of your head. When open, this is what connects us to spirit.

Dark Spirits - Evil Spirits
These are earthbound spirits, or ghosts who choose to live in the dark realm, or were created in the dark realm.

Demon
An evil spirit, ghost or devil associate. Thought to be able to possess a person or an object.

Elemental
A spirit that is harmonious with the elements water, air, fire and earth.

EMF Meter - Electromagnetic Field Detector/ Meter
A piece of equipment adapted to the field of ghost/spirit investigation. The meter measures variations in electromagnetic fields around you.

ESP/Extra Sensory Perception
This is the ability to receive information that is sensed/seen with your mind. This is not done through recognized physical senses.

Essence
What each of us is made up of; what is at the base of each of us, our soul.

EVP or Electronic Voice Phenomena
When using a recording device, voices or sounds captured and interpreted to be otherworldly.

Flashlight Test
Two flashlights are turned to the point they are almost on. Each flash light is typically one for yes and one for no. Questions are asked aloud. Spirit then turns on the appropriate flashlight as a responding answer. There is much debate about this test/using this sort of flashlight. Flashlights with push button activation for on/off, dispel the idea of battery connection being too close, unlike the other style flashlight. For the push button type, the test does not change.

Ghost Box
A modified portable radio used to make contact with spirits.
The radio is broken, or modified, so that it does not stay on
one band, it continually scans all the bands.

Laser Grid
These come in many sizes, and depend on wants-and-needs.
My experience is with a small flashlight size for investigations.
The grid, usually green colored, is the most visible color of laser.
The grid can be projected down hallways, on flat walls or to
light-up a section of a room. The grid will show movement as
spirit moves through it. Dots of the grid will disappear as
movement happens. You may also see full shapes or a solid
mass.

Medium
See Clairvoyant.

Mind's Eye
Receiving mental images or pictures in your mind. Also referred
to as the Third Eye.

Motion Detector
A device, when placed strategically, will make a noise/sound to
let you know there has been movement in the area. These are
often placed in a location you are not currently investigating. It
allows you to monitor two, or more, locations at once,
depending on how many you use.

Oils to Anoint
Several different types of oils may be used for anointing.
Essential oils, holy or blessed oils, and oils of the earth such as
olive oil. These oils can be used to anoint a person, place and/or
object. Reasons to anoint are vast—in rituals and religious
ceremonies for thousands of years, for rites of passage, and for
blessings of places or things.

Open
Connecting with the spirit world by opening up the crown of
your head or Third Eye.

Portal
Other names include gateways or doorways. These all do the
same thing: they open entryways from one realm/vibrational
plane to another. Openings may allow any sort of spirit, ghost,
demon, etc., to pass through.

REM Pod
This piece of equipment is designed specifically for paranormal
research/investigating. The antenna on its circular shape covers
360 degrees. It detects/picks-up disturbances in energy. Around
the top, are colored lights that illuminate when the energy near
the REM Pod is disturbed. An alarm/noise will also sound at
the time of the disturbance; that makes this tool useful to use in
rooms which you are currently not.

Sage/Saging/Smudging
A cleansing technique with Native American roots. Dried herbs,
bark, and/or sweet grass (bundled or loose) is burned for
purification. While burning any of these, prayers of your choice
may be said. Also during this time, keep your intentions pure,
positive, and loving.

Salt
Use to keep spirit out during a smudge or saging. The area you
are cleansing is saged or smudged first, and as you exit the area,
you salt to close the room off. It is a boundary protector—spirit
cannot pass over the salt. It is also said that salt can absorb
psychic energy. May people have a salt preference, I use
common house salt; any sort of salt will work

Spirit Attachment
A spirit, good or bad, attaches its soul to a living being, an animal or object.

Spirit Box
See Ghost Box.

The Knowing/Knowing
Having an understanding of things, that you would not have any way of knowing.

Third Eye/Mind's Eye
Imaginary/invisible eye in your forehead area thought to give you perception beyond ordinary sight.

Transcendental
In the spiritual/metaphysical world, beyond the ordinary or common experience or belief.

Tune In
See Open.

Veil
A way of covering a person, place or thing, and protecting it from spiritual attack, attachment or from being bothered.

Vibrational Plane
There are many planes that coexist, operated by the different rates of vibration.

Wendigo
A cannibal, monster or evil spirit. The Cree Indian translation of the word is "evil that devours." Can possess humans.

NOTES